Praise for *Rise and Climb*

"A testament to the fact that tough times don't last forever but the strength you build during those times can persist. Ben Barbic offers a shining example of how to find purpose in the pain, and it's an inspiring book for anyone who wants to live a life of intention and resilience."

—Amy Morin, author of *13 Things Mentally Strong People Don't Do*

"A powerful reminder that our greatest wounds can become the very source of our strength. Ben Barbic doesn't just tell his story—he hands us a blueprint for transforming pain into purpose. Raw, real, and profoundly human."

—Robert Lufkin, MD, *New York Times* bestselling author of *Lies I Taught in Medical School*

"I know *Rise and Climb* will change many lives. It's authentic, raw, and full of lived truth. Ben Barbic proves that real transformation isn't theory—it's daily practice."

—Marc Reklau, author of *30 Days: Change Your Habits, Change Your Life*

"A coming-of-age story packed with real-world lessons that leave you smiling, thinking, and turning every page. Holden Caulfield's got nothing on Ben Barbic—this one's the real thing."

—Zack Reed, owner of Rebel Sound Records and former A&R at VP Records

"*Rise and Climb* isn't a 'feel-good' self-help pep talk; it's a blueprint written in callouses and consequences."

—Manning Sumner, founder & CEO, Legacy & NO DAYS OFF

"Life doesn't come with a soundtrack, but perhaps it should. In his compelling book, Ben Barbic argues that music is far more than entertainment—it is a vital tool for survival. Through powerful storytelling and keen insight, Barbic reveals how a familiar song can ground us, a beat can give us courage, and a lyric can articulate our deepest pain when words fail. This is a moving exploration of how, no matter how difficult the path, and how painful our life experience has been, music has the unique power to carve out a space of normalcy and make the unbearable, bearable."

—Keith Rowe, Reggae legend, Keith & Tex ("Stop That Train")

"An inspirational work that reminds us to be persistent in our pursuit of greatness. Nothing that is worth doing is ever easy. Ben's personal story reinforces that in life things happen for us and not to us. When we adopt that frame of mind and perspective, we grow and learn from setbacks and failures, rather than allowing them to break us. If you want to be inspired, read this book."

—Dr. Nathan S. Bryan, scientist and author of *The Secret of Nitric Oxide*

"An uplifting guide that gives readers real tools to grow and stay inspired. Ben's honest, motivating voice makes the book powerful and genuinely transformative."

—E.N Young, Reggae producer and artist

"Breaking my back was something I had to overcome. It taught me how to go on and made me better than before. *Rise and Climb* is a lesson in perseverance for all of us."

—Kenny Roberts, first American to win a 500cc Grand Prix World Championship, three-time world champion, and motorcycle racing legend

"An enjoyable 'hero's journey' for any level of reader. Powerful, funny, and very well written. Ben Barbic is utterly fearless in telling his life's story. I feel overjoyed to get to know a man I've worked with only a handful of times with this depth of perspective. I'm so excited to hear the new music that comes from him now!"

—Dan Konopka, drummer of Grammy Award–winning band OK Go

"*Rise and Climb* powerfully captures Ben's unwavering commitment to personal growth—a pursuit in which he consistently excels. As a close friend, I can say his outstanding work ethic and drive toward excellence are matched by a deep sense of service and compassion. Ben embodies the timeless truth that lifting others not only moves the world forward but also gives lasting meaning and purpose to those who choose that path."

—Dino Campanella, drummer and keyboardist of Dredg

Rise & Climb

Rise & Climb

Finding Purpose Through Pain

Ben Barbic

Skyhorse Publishing

Skyhorse Publishing books may be purchased in bulk at special discounts for sales promotion, corporate gifts, fund-raising, or educational purposes. Special editions can also be created to specifications. For details, contact the Special Sales Department, Skyhorse Publishing, 307 Fifth Avenue, 4th Floor, New York, NY 10016 or info@skyhorsepublishing.com.

Visit our website at www.skyhorsepublishing.com.

Please follow our publisher Tony Lyons on Instagram @tonylyonsisuncertain.

10 9 8 7 6 5 4 3 2 1

Library of Congress Cataloging-in-Publication Data is available on file.

Cover design by David Ter-Avanesyan
Cover image courtesy of the author

Print ISBN: 978-1-5107-8608-0
Ebook ISBN: 978-1-5107-8609-7

Printed in the United States of America

This book is dedicated to my family—past, present, and future. To those before me whom I still carry in my heart. To those who currently bring me strength when I am at my weakest. And to those in the future who I hope will find value and inspiration from the words in the coming pages.

Please visit https://www.risenclimb.com/trace for the exclusive musical soundtrack, photos, and videos to enhance your Rise and Climb Experience.

CONTENTS

INTRODUCTION

I START EARLY. USUALLY, a few hours before dawn. Before the world can ask anything of me, I show up for myself and nurture my progress on multiple fronts. It took me seventeen years to get to where I am now. Seventeen years of daily progress and rising every morning with purpose. I now have a book publishing deal and a literary agent, and the soundtrack to this book is being released through Rebel Sound Records. I am the cofounder of a small real estate brokerage called Barbic Real Estate Group, which I started with my father. I have also traveled the world, all because of the music that I made in my basement studio. I have a twenty-three-year-old son, a thirteen-year-old daughter, and a wife I have been married to for fourteen years. But seventeen years ago, everything was the opposite of now. Everything was chaos and dysfunction. I was sinking fast. It took a fateful night on my twenty-eighth birthday while sitting in a jail cell—again—for me to flip my life around and make this change.

This change wasn't easy. I had to remodel nearly every aspect of my life. I started by removing bad habits, then replacing them with good ones. One by one and day by day, things changed. I found joy in forward progress. I craved the process. While writing, I saw themes in my life that were my consistent challenges. I found lessons that could be shared and explained. Some are mistakes, setbacks, and failures. Some are wins and successes on a large scale. More than anything, I found a thread of resilience through my life. I am going to be quite honest and revealing because, through open dialogue, we can learn more about ourselves and those around us.

We all face the roller coaster known as life. *Rise and Climb: Finding Purpose Through Pain* is a raw account of my life and what I gained on my journey. It explains how early on I stumbled and got lost in the difficult moments, but with time, how I learned to find the pieces of guidance within the pain and struggle. I will show you how I turned my pain into fuel and, in my ever-increasing search for purpose, completely transformed my life. No matter your age, whether you're at a rock-bottom moment yourself or thriving in your career and currently at the top, the words in the coming pages are intended to resonate and help you on your journey.

We all have areas of our lives that could use a tune-up. Sometimes, many areas could use a complete rebuild. *Rise and Climb* is about living the life you want and getting the most out of your short amount of time on the planet. It is meant to inspire you to rise every day, excited for what's ahead, and climb in many aspects of life.

Climb boldly. Rise daily. Find your purpose in the pain.

CHAPTER 1

ON THE ROAD AGAIN

THE FIRST FIVE YEARS of my life were like a dream. My dad was a professional motorcycle racer, and my parents owned multiple motorcycle dealerships. I would ride around in the dirt behind the shops on my three-wheel dirt bike, hang out with the employees, and daydream on the showroom floor. I was a miniature racer in the making and had the thrill gene in my blood.

We lived in the Santa Cruz Mountains, surrounded by hundreds of towering redwood trees. The trees were like skyscrapers, many over ten stories tall. We lived in a little old house, where racers, mechanics, friends, and associates from the shop were always present, giving it incredible energy—it was a life outside the norms of suit-and-tie cubicle life.

Our garage was filled with motorcycle trophies my dad won from his years of professional motorcycle racing. He qualified ninth at Daytona in 1978, right behind road racing legend Kenny Roberts. Unfortunately, he had a massive crash in a race where he lost traction and smashed into the guardrail at a very high speed. He lost his spleen, ending his racing career, but returned for a final race after the crash. It was the only road race of his I attended, but I was too young to remember. I do remember trophies lining the walls, though. To a little kid, it seemed like millions of them. I think my sense of him doing something big came from seeing all the wins. It was my first sense of greatness—the feeling that you push for excellence in life.

By the time he was nineteen, my pops had become such a sought-after mechanic that he was ready to open his own shop. Yamaha was the only company willing to take a chance and give him a motorcycle dealership license, so "Yamaha of San Jose" was born. My mom moved out to California from Buffalo, New York, in the mid-1970s—when she met my dad—and they ran the shops for a while before I was born. In one of the first pictures of me, I'm on a motorcycle. The bikes were loud, and the sound of revving engines was constant. Also, two-stroke motors have a strong, distinct smell as they burn fuel, and I wouldn't be surprised if they helped me fall asleep as a baby. The chaos and power of a gasoline motor has always calmed me—it's familiar.

We had an orange 1973 Dodge van that we rolled in, usually with bikes in the back. It even had two sleeping bunks with orange 1970s carpet for when my dad would travel around the country to do professional motorcycle racing. In that playground known as "The Van," I distinctly remember driving while listening to Willie Nelson's "On the Road Again." I was amazed at the song. I would stare at the *Honeysuckle Rose* album with the tour bus on the cover and get lost in the music as we drove around San Jose. My life was joy-filled, and that song perfectly aligned with my life in this counterculture. "On the Road Again" was the soundtrack of my early years. I wanted to hear that song every time we got in the van. As an only child, I had enough people and excitement around me to never feel alone. It felt like the world was a playground—until I turned five.

In July 1985, I was at my cousin's house in Santa Cruz. While running through his kitchen, I heard, "There is a forest fire in the Santa Cruz Mountains." I stopped and looked up, stunned, at the TV as footage of acres of mountains burned above Lexington Reservoir, nearing my family's home. It felt like this evil demon energy was killing everything in its path. I stood there, cemented to the floor, watching the TV with the first dark feeling of my childhood. It was a feeling I would never forget. This inferno of evil was attacking my world. My father raced to my cousin's and said they weren't letting any cars up the mountain. He asked me what I wanted him to grab if they let him through, and for some reason, I told him to get my Knight Rider car. As I watched him drive away to grab whatever he could, I kept picturing him walking through the house one last time, frantically collecting whatever seemed to matter while the walls were burning around him. I felt the chaos of my imagined scenarios. My dad choosing what to take and what we would never see again.

When life comes down to collecting what you can in only minutes and you're panic stricken, it's about the memories, the pictures. He saved a few other items he could fit in the van, but that was about it. He did grab my Knight Rider car. Other than that, I lost all I had: toys, house, and comfort zone—all was lost. Dad returned from the mountains, and everything we owned now fit in the back of that orange van. Our house and property were destroyed.

About a week later, we drove up to the property, and it was like seeing a war zone. Embers were still burning in spots, and smoke was rising. The smell was something that became engrained in my soul. A house fire smells so different from a wood fire. Something so haunting and repulsive. We walked around, and I felt a sense of doom. There were no walls, ceilings, or roof. Plants, toys, motorcycle trophies, records—anything that resembled our stuff was gone. All that remained were some coins in a pot that had turned to molten metal and fused together.

I smiled as my mom took pictures of the remains of our home. These pictures of me smiling are a reminder that young children are not prepared to deal with trauma and tragedy. I had no idea how to reference this in my young life. I also had no idea what this meant. I did feel like the fire was a spirit—an evil spirit—that violently devoured everything. It scared me, and my only reaction was awkwardly smiling, trying not to upset it anymore. I hoped I could find something of mine that remained, but there was nothing.

Around where our garage once stood, we found one thing the fire couldn't destroy. Although the paint had been burned off them, the barbells and weight plates remained recognizable and had kept their shape. In preservation mode, we picked up the weights and loaded them in the van. The fire couldn't take them. Iron is tough. The building and everything else—completely gone. But they survived. Those weights, like the David Hasselhoff figure from inside my Knight Rider car, have stayed with me—over forty years later.

As we drove away, I felt that our home was no longer a place of safety but a place of trauma and violence. It was a place that couldn't be trusted. The fire had raged up the hillside, devouring our home in an inferno—we were at the mercy of its moves. It chose us to torment. Life was changing. I was losing the only world I knew.

In the aftermath of the fire, my parents, thirty-six years old at the time, were in survival mode and couldn't keep an eye on the motorcycle business. While they were distracted, the store manager embezzled a substantial amount of money, and they couldn't keep things afloat. We lost all the stores shortly after.

I have vivid memories of returning to the place of my childhood joy and watching all the bikes leave, looking at the empty shelves once filled with helmets, shirts, motorcycle pants, and endless accessories. When my dad locked the door for the final time, I was there. It was just the two of us as he locked away the world we knew. This was more than losing the stores. We turned away from the culture. It was too hard to face. My father lost all he had dreamed of since he opened his motorcycle business at nineteen. We had no safety net—no place to escape to. The flames were attacking from all around. An evil force was stripping us of our world. We were now without a home, and my parents were out of work.

Finding Purpose Through Pain

There will be times in your life when everything changes in an instant. The world you knew could be taken from you without any warning—and these moments don't ask for your permission. The trauma doesn't always look like pain immediately—it could show up as confusion, silence, or a forced smile while standing amid the ashes. But it will shape you. If you face it and work with it, it can help to forge your strength. What's lost in the fire can never be replaced, but what is born in that fire can never be destroyed.

You will lose things—homes, dreams, businesses, and people. I lost everything when our family home burned down, leaving only molten coins and rusted weights and barbells. Remember that destruction is not the end; it's the ignition point of a new beginning if we make it so.

CHAPTER 2

IT'S SO EASY

WE MOVED INTO MY grandparents' small apartment on Branham Lane in San Jose. They had lived there since they followed my mom out to California after I was born. The time I spent there felt like I was always waiting to go home and return to the life I knew. I felt lost in a familiar place.

The apartment complex let a local church set up a donation drop-off for our family because we had only the clothes we wore, nothing else. It was uncomfortable as a six-year-old to be the recipient of things you would find at a donation center. Weird items that people no longer needed piled up: used clothes, dinnerware, toys, and even small kitchen appliances. Everything we were given had a feeling of the past. I received a stack of *Unknown Soldier* comics. They were frightening. Clothes and appliances were a decade past their desirability range—though strangely, we kept many items for years. All these years later, my parents still have the 1970s yellow Air Pop popcorn maker someone donated. It sounds like an air horn and brings me back every time it's used.

The local television stations came by on donation day to interview us. It was a twisted dream—getting so much attention at a sad time. I wasn't sure if people cared or if they just liked to hear about how messed up things get. We were in the paper, too, and I felt conflicting emotions with the media's intent. This wasn't attention for something positive. It was attention for something incredibly negative—something terrible we had gone through. To this day, when disaster victims are interviewed, it makes me feel uneasy. I can relate, and it's not a time when I would want to go on TV and answer "What happened?" with a damn microphone in my face—but there is something to getting attention. The news team interviewed me. They asked me what donations I got. My young self enthusiastically said, "I got two alarm clocks!" My moment of fame in a lost child's young life.

Someone graciously donated a 1973 Road Ranger travel trailer for us to live in. Without hesitation, we moved out of my grandparents' apartment and towed the trailer to Saratoga Springs—a campground in the Saratoga Hills. The first few days were fun—it felt like we were camping. Then reality set in. I was about to enter first grade.

I was starting at St. Mary's School in Los Gatos, California, and my home life could not even be called "home life"—more of a deranged nomadic existence. Getting ready for school in a campground felt wrong. Driving there was even more so. I loved the drive in the van—it was a little taste of what used to be. I could pretend that things were still OK. On the road, life felt normal. But then my new life couldn't be hidden any longer. Here comes the orange van dropping off camper Ben in downtown Los Gatos while all the Mercedes Benzes and Suburbans were dropping off kids, smiling and seemingly all familiar with each other. I had never seen life like this. I didn't know wealth. I never spent time in downtown Los Gatos. Also, where I lived and what my parents did for a living weren't questions I could answer.

After a few months we moved the trailer back to our property in the Santa Cruz Mountains—where our home once stood. It wasn't the same; it still smelled like a campsite fire pit everywhere, and the redwoods around the trailer were all burned and covered in ash. The bark became a charcoal that I could break off and write with. These trees, like the weights from my garage, survived. The trauma was all around, though. The soul and beauty were gone. All the small trees and bushes were dead. Nothing was green or even alive. If I looked up, I could see that the tops of the redwoods were still alive. They were traumatized, but like me, they survived. The fire didn't kill them, but they would always carry the scars.

My family and I lived in that trailer for two years. We had no power, running water, or plumbing. My dad borrowed a small generator to power a few things and ran a pipe down the hillside to a cesspool he dug by hand, so we had somewhere to put the waste. Eventually we got running water, and I distinctly remember when we got clearance to put up a temporary electrical pole. The simple things are anything but simple—food, water, shelter, and power. For me, the privilege of having power never goes unnoticed.

The Road Ranger was just a trailer, no bigger than a large pickup truck. I got the top sleeping bunk, and my folks got the bottom bunk. The trailer was old and had this odd smell like a time capsule of years gone by. It felt unwanted and used—like a terrible one-star hotel.

I have blocked most of my memories from this time, so I can barely recall the two years we spent living inside the trailer. My parents desperately did whatever they could to rebuild our lives. My dad worked any jobs he could. The only motorcycle left was a Yamaha Seca that sat outside the trailer, getting weathered by the elements but never ridden. A sad, lingering reminder of the joy of the past.

At a county fair at the school up the street from our property, they had kittens for sale. I convinced my parents to get one, and I was so excited. I named him Smokey. He was black and white, and the name seemed fitting. A few weeks later, I was sitting on the built-in couch in the trailer watching cartoons when I heard a faint meow outside the small metal screen door. Something wasn't right. Smokey had what looked like an M&M hanging on his face. As I got closer, I saw that his eyeball was hanging out of his head. I don't know where my parents were when this happened, but it seemed like a personal moment of darkness. I remember bending down at the metal screen door and looking at Smokey's head, with its broken bones and massive trauma. I stared at him, repulsed by his condition and wanting to hold him. As I knelt, frozen, I felt death was near. I could feel the evil force creeping in. My mom finally came around and picked him up to take him to the vet. He was beyond healing—Smokey died.

This encounter with death was terrifying. Life seemed like a cruel series of painful experiences. I could not deal with the pain the world was giving me. I needed something to escape into. I needed something to remove me from this world of constant loss and negative experiences.

My parents bought me a Casio keyboard for Christmas. This was my first electronic musical instrument. It was like a friend. It played music and let me participate. There were little cartridges you could insert into the keyboard, then select the song and play along. It was one of the first MIDI sequence-playing instruments. I put the keyboard on the little table in the trailer and got lost in the music, listening and playing along to the theme to "Star Wars," "Amazing Grace," and other songs. I could, on a primitive level, make music and control it. I loved the freedom it gave me. It was an escape in a trailer filled with emotional stress and pain—there was hope in this. In the world of music, the musical space was my own. I was able to create the world I wanted, not the other way around. I could take some of the trauma and release it through the keys. I could harness the flames, turning them into fuel instead of letting them destroy me.

I came from a motorcycle shop, had my house burned down, lived in a trailer, and my parents were frantically looking for work. I attended a Catholic school in downtown Los Gatos with mostly upper-middle-class and upper-class families. Down the street was a Lamborghini dealership, a corner candy store, and luxury cars everywhere. Most other kids had siblings, big houses, stay-at-home moms, and fathers with stable jobs. Our car was still an orange van that had just had the lettering taken off the side that said YAMAHA OF SAN JOSE. Except the paint was darker than the rest of the van, so you could still see it. I would get dropped off, usually late, and it was embarrassing. It felt like a different world at school—I was an outsider looking in.

I'm not pretending that my story matches what some in this world must endure—families experiencing war, extreme violence, hunger, illness, and more. I'm saying that in Silicon Valley, the Bay Area of California, in the 1980s and '90s, when tech wealth was taking off, I was outside that world of stability, looking in. For many years, I watched my classmates live in wealth, routines, and safety nets while I was merely surviving. It frustrated me to be so unplugged in a place that felt so connected. But I learned to embrace it, and that contrast shaped me and gave me my edge. I want to respect and acknowledge the extreme struggles of many in this world while telling my story.

My best memory was when my school installed a new play structure. My dad helped take down the old one, and we kept the materials and built a tree fort out of the old wood. I had a two-story tree house between three redwood trees. I didn't give a shit about being in a trailer. I had a better tree house than all of my classmates. We had taken the school's trash—old wood—and made something out of it. We turned the "unwanted" into a place to dream—something I could trust. I would sit in the tree house between those three burnt redwood trees and feel safe. They survived, like me. There was a calmness that I wouldn't know anywhere else. This place was special to me. It stood firm for over twenty years—eventually, the tree house fell as the trees grew too tall and robust. The now gigantic trees still show the wounds of the past, and the fallen wood remains at the base of those trees, covered by the growth of the forest.

The days at the shop were drifting further into my fading memories. My identity as a motorcycle kid was in the past. There was no evidence that it had existed—except for the van and my lunch bags for school. I felt uncomfortable eating peanut butter and jelly sandwiches from old paper bags with YAMAHA OF SAN JOSE on them for my lunch. In contrast, the other kids ate these glorious lunches with cinnamon rolls and warm McDonald's on a "hot lunch" day. I would eat the BBQ sauce packets on McDonald's Day to feel like I was a part of it. I felt different, but I also liked it. I didn't want to be the same. The same seemed dull—like a subdivision where all the houses were the same size, shape, and color. I would rather be outside that—even if my roof was leaky.

I didn't have motorcycles anymore—that ship had sailed. But, now six, I was introduced to recording. I figured out that you could record if you put tape on the edge of a cassette tape, covering the little holes. I entered the world of music and recording the first time I hit the RECORD button. I would take a tape deck and record myself singing, talking, and whatever else music-related—I even made little radio shows with my boombox. I loved the permanence of the recording. I could live beyond the moment, and I could interact with it. There is something fascinating about moments frozen in time in an audio recording. Holding on to these moments brought me comfort. Recording became my place to go—vital to my survival as the years passed.

Down the street from our property was a kid the same age as me. He had a house with a pool, so I would spend a lot of time there. He had the Guns N' Roses *Appetite for Destruction* tape, and the song "It's So Easy" felt so real to me. It spoke to me like "On the Road Again" had a few years earlier. When Axl Rose's lyrics dropped, it felt like a piece of the motorcycle shop was back in my soul. Amid the heavy vocals and use of the word "fuck," somehow, a bit of my world returned. I felt alive again for the first time since all the destruction. The energy of "It's So Easy" was what I was feeling. I wanted to stay in the world of this music, not my real life.

Finding Purpose Through Pain

There could come a time when your life no longer feels like your own. Your comfort and self-esteem could be stripped away as you are forced to start over with secondhand clothes, a donated shelter, and a version of yourself you barely recognize. I vividly remember standing in front of the cameras with my two alarm clocks, smiling for the TV crew. It wasn't happiness, it was discomfort and confusion, as I suddenly became the recipient of charity. It might feel like you've fallen too far to ever climb out of it. But survival itself is its own form of strength. It helps to grow your ability to endure.

Sometimes the pain hits hardest in seemingly simple moments: the lunch bag containing far less than your classmates have to eat, the embarrassing drop-off in an old car, or the look in someone's eyes that says you don't belong. Remember in these trying moments that you are not less, you are just in the initial phase of becoming more.

When everything outside you feels broken, you must find that which brings you peace inside. That can be art, music, sport, weightlifting, or writing; find something that gives you that feeling of escape and control. Creativity can be a method of survival, giving you the power to turn your pain into fuel and build something from the ashes. Even the smallest spark of inspiration can provide you with safety when the world offers you none. Hold it sacred.

CHAPTER 3

APPLE JUICE WITH LEAVES

We were nearly broke, contemplating picking up and leaving the Bay Area in a soul-crushing defeat. We had tried to build our house back on the property but were struggling financially. One day, my parents decided to do whatever it took to complete the house. They worked jobs they hated at full throttle, and time went by slowly in the trailer until the home was completed.

We left the trailer for the last time and stepped into something that felt like magic—a brand-new home built just for us and mostly by us. It was fresh, untouched, and finally ours. I'd sit at my desk in school, daydreaming about when the bell would ring so I could run back to that new space. It felt safe. Loving. Normal—at least *my* version of normal.

It was during this quiet stretch of stability that I wrote my first song. I was seven years old, sitting at the dining room table, staring at a glass bottle of Martinelli's Apple Juice with its leafy top. I felt something I hadn't felt in a long time: calm. No chaos. No sadness. Just stillness—and in that stillness, melody.

Out of nowhere, a jingle started forming in my mind, carried on the cadence of "On Top of Spaghetti" by the great Mr. Snuffleupagus. Without effort, it poured out:

I found a can of apple juice
All covered with leaves
I read the label; it said Martinelli's
I twisted the cap and drank it down slow
I threw it away
I miss it so.

"Apple Juice with Leaves"

The music was waking up. So was I. I gave meaning to the simplest act—drinking juice—and unknowingly tapped into something powerful: my voice. I didn't realize it yet, but this soundtrack in my mind had always been there. It had just been buried under the noise. Now, in this new house, it started to come alive.

I was turning everything into a song. Back then, we had landlines and answering machines, and I sang our voice message to the melody of Stevie Wonder's "I Just Called to Say I Love You." That jingle became my first public performance—every time someone called, they heard it.

You just called to say . . .
I'm sorry I missed your call
Please leave your name and your number
After the beep
Thanks, Bye

"You Just Called"

Our garage contained leftover items from the shop days. No bikes, just random parts that would never get used. My dad would have me go to the garage to lift weights on a bench he had bought—to a seven-year-old, it seemed massive. It was a Marcy bench from the late 1980s, and it adjusted, allowing you to do incline presses. I could barely do the bar on the bench press—and this was a standard bar, not an Olympic—but he helped my unsteady arms get some reps as I learned how to balance the weight. The bar I held had withstood the fire and was still rusted from enduring the flames—same with all the plates. After every lift, the bar became a little easier to hold as the rust mixed with the sweat from our hands to help clean it off.

Surrounded by a haunting memory of that past that no longer was, we shared some of the only time we had together then, among those weights. There I was, a seven-year-old, lifting weights and connecting with my father, while encompassed from every direction by reminders of our previous life. Here lies the power of this situation. We were creating something magical amid that chaos. We were putting all our energy into the lifts. After the workouts, I would go inside our new house, out of the abyss of the past, and feel amazing. The seed was planted. We no longer rode motorcycles—weightlifting was now a standard in my life.

Weightlifting was present in my blood; my family has lifted weights for generations. Way before it was considered cool, my grandfather and all his brothers lifted and even competed in bodybuilding. My grandfather's brother was in the 1953 Mr. Universe contest in London. I have a picture of him on stage standing next to Sean Connery, who also competed. My dad and his two brothers continued the tradition, and all three are strong—even into their sixties and beyond.

The day before my tenth birthday, the World Series was on TV. I had my first birthday slumber party in the new home the weekend before. My absolute favorite team, the Oakland A's, was about to play the Bay Area team, the Giants, in the Bay Bridge Series. My grandparents and I were all set up in their apartment to watch the game. My parents were going to come by after work and we had dinner ready with the kitchen table moved to the living room, so we didn't miss any of it. I was happy.

It was 5:04 p.m. on October 17, 1989. The apartment shook violently right as the game announced the starting lineups. The TV flickered and then went black. Everything around the room started falling to the ground. My grandfather, grandmother, and I ran to a doorway and thought their second-floor apartment would crash down to the lower unit—the violence had returned. The evil feeling returned. The flames were back.

After the shaking stopped, we ran outside. All the water from the community pool had poured out onto the walkways. Hundreds of people were standing in the pathways between the buildings, a look of shock filling our faces.

The extent of the damage started rolling in, and we found out the Cypress Structure—a double-decker highway in Oakland—had collapsed, killing many. The Bay Bridge had partly collapsed, as had buildings in the Marina District of San Francisco. My parents weren't with me, so I didn't know if they were okay—there were no cell phones then.

Eventually my parents arrived, and while listening to the radio, we heard we couldn't go up Highway 17 to our house. We didn't know much more than that, but again, that feeling of our home potentially being damaged came into our minds. On the news, we also heard that the earthquake was where our newly built house was. They called it the Loma Prieta earthquake. And guess what school we lived directly behind? Loma Prieta. It was a long night of unknowns as we waited for permission to see that potential damage.

The drive up the mountain to check on our home felt like déjà vu. I was frightened. The world was becoming a place of evil. Aftershocks were a constant threat, and I was anxious about being under an overpass while another earthquake occurred—worried I would be taken out. Finally, the highway patrol stopped us under an overpass at a checkpoint and, after some discussion, let us up the mountain. We had no idea what awaited us as we got closer to our house. Only four years earlier, we had made this same drive, anxiously waiting to see what remained of our home. I couldn't go through this again.

When we arrived at our house, we could see the garage door had been ripped off its rails and was lurching forward. All the shelving in the garage holding the parts from the motorcycle store had collapsed violently, causing the garage door to break off. It looked as if a semi-truck had hit it. Before leaving the car, my parents and I shared worried looks, knowing what awaited us inside. In the kitchen, the plates and glasses were all broken. In the living room, all the fish from my ten-gallon tank were dead on the ground, lying among shards of shattered glass. My room didn't feel like my room. It felt like a mob of robbers had ripped everything apart. This room, which I had dreamed of for so long and loved having, was now a place of evil. Most importantly, our house had moved off its foundation, making it uninhabitable.

As I walked around the house, I could feel the violence that once again had ravaged our home. Everywhere we looked was destruction. I remember feeling like it wasn't our house. It felt like a horror movie, and the soul was stripped out of what a few days earlier had been a place of celebration and newfound joy in the home we had built. I walked past my birthday presents, still sitting in the living room. Those disheveled gifts were a slap-in-the-face reminder that this earthquake had instantly taken the joy from me. My new fantasy life of happiness and stability was over just as it had begun. This beautiful new home was now out of touch, out of reach—and so was my happiness. My soundtrack stopped again. My world came crashing down—literally and figuratively. This was my birthday, October 18, 1989—the day I turned ten.

Everyone at my school had the same life as the day before—but mine was different. My life was messed up once again. I related to no one. Some kids had various forms of trauma, but what type of unusual existence was this? Now, I lived in a world utterly different from the "On the Road Again" motorcycle shop days. I remember some kids at school said they were at soccer practice during the earthquake and thought it was fun. That was it, fucking fun! At that moment, more than any other, I realized how different I was. I wasn't like them. I didn't belong. I was alone. No other kid in my class had more than some dishes and TVs fall in the quake, but we lost everything we had just built. I felt like I had lost control and was scared. Scared of the unknown that awaited me next. I thought death must be next. I couldn't trust the world around me, so I probably couldn't count on good health, either.

My first sign of anxiety came as I sat in a chair on the patio of our destroyed home. I started feeling like something was wrong with my heart. I felt like I was dying. I never spoke of this to my parents—I was too scared to acknowledge what had happened. I never told anyone until this writing, but the anxiety that became my constant companion started to reveal itself that day. My body was reacting to the trauma. I didn't know it then, but this was just the beginning.

We moved to an apartment in Los Gatos across from Vasona Park. Nothing about this time felt right. So, I claimed an area in a tree in the far corner of the complex, where I had a very primitive tree fort. The manager told me the day after I had created my space to stop going over to the tree. The tree wasn't for use—it was ornamental only. I felt I had no place to go, no escape. I couldn't build a place for me.

Our neighbor in the mountains, whose home had also been destroyed in the earthquake, was in temporary housing. He came over to spend the night and brought some cassette tapes. He was one of the only people to enter that apartment—struggling similarly. He pulled out an album called *Stone Cold Rhymin'*. It appeared old-school in design, so I figured it was some old 1950s or '60s music—I had low expectations. We popped it in my General Electric boombox. Boom! I couldn't have been more wrong. What I heard changed what I had known about music and what music was capable of. "Bust a Move" was infectious. Young MC's flow, cadence, and swagger made me happy while the music played. "Fastest Rhyme" was perfect for me, a rapid-fire, lyrically chaotic gem that captivated me. I kept thinking about that music and how it made me feel alive. It was a world within the sound that I could escape to. The next day, my mom took me to the Wherehouse record store, and I bought the tape.

I put the tape in my new Sony Sports Walkman and found my thing. This world of music was me. I wanted to be inside of the music—a part of it. To float in the dream world that is sound. Pressing play on the rubberized green PLAY button was my drug, how I got high—even when thinking about it now. This device marked the beginning of my journey to the inner world of music, where everything else fades away. I didn't want to leave this world. Over thirty years later, the space of the headphones is still my favorite—and now, I most definitely participate.

Finding Purpose Through Pain

You can be tested in almost unbelievable ways. You can taste the euphoria of success and be living your dreams, only to have them taken away from you. Your inner soundtrack can be singing beautiful songs, only to have your joy silenced. Just days after celebrating my tenth birthday with friends in our newly built home, the violent shaking of the Loma Prieta earthquake took away the joy of that safe haven and turned it into another scene of trauma and loss. These are the moments of truly being tested. When everything crumbles down, that is the moment of decision. Can you rebuild again? Can you flip your mentality to push forward, no matter what? Can you find that mindset inside that will endure no matter what is thrown at you?

In these most difficult tests, when you're faced with the multiple setbacks, you must double down on what gives you strength. Create outlets for fitness and sports, and they must be given extra fuel. Persistently push each day forward. There can be residual effects from trauma. There can be anxiety, PTSD, or countless other aftermaths of life's struggles. I can still vividly recall sitting quietly on the patio of our earthquake-damaged house, overwhelmed with anxiety and convinced something was wrong with my heart. The inner wounds I faced became internalized fear. What I didn't know then was how to understand what was happening, acknowledge it, and keep moving forward. Do not succumb to chaos. Find that inner flame of hope, no matter how faint, and embrace the moment to help you build and grow. The gifts of struggle can give you superpowers as you go through life.

CHAPTER 4

EVERYTHING'S GONNA BE ALRIGHT

I STARTED HAVING PANIC attacks at around eleven years old. Bad events were happening out of nowhere—I had no control. I remember sitting in my classroom at St. Mary's and feeling a recurring sense of not belonging, as if I were alone while surrounded by people, completely disconnected. I looked out the classroom door and felt the urge to get out of my seat and run. Suddenly, I couldn't breathe. I thought I was about to die at my desk. I told the teacher I was sick and walked down to the nurse's office, where they told me to lie down. I stared at the ceiling, thinking this was the end. I remember the secretary was listening to "Achy Breaky Heart" by Billy Ray Cyrus while I was lying there, thinking I was dying. I couldn't believe this was the song I had to hear as I lay there dying, and they were talking about how handsome Billy Ray's hair was. Why did they not seem to care? The feelings of evil I had experienced before the fire and earthquake were now in my soul. I felt the inner flames attacking—fire from within. The danger was now inside.

After what felt like hours, my parents arrived and took me to the doctor. The doctor had me breathe into a paper lunch bag and told me I was hyperventilating—having a panic attack. I went home from there, paper bag in hand, not wanting to let my new safety net out of my hands. A paper lunch bag and I linked up really close from there. Over the next few months, it was my ever-present buddy. Ben now rolled everywhere with a brown paper bag of "snacks"—but I was never hungry.

When not in that terror dome known as school, I would record my voice over music or make little one-person radio shows. I would play them back and analyze how they sounded. I used the recordings to keep me company and escape. A positive outcome of my escape method was that I was getting used to hearing my voice on the mic. At ten years old, I developed a familiarity with the microphone and how my voice sounded when playing it back after recording.

I was developing other skills too. While still in the apartment, my mom occasionally included me in her work outings. She would take me to the flea market on the weekends as she went from vendor to vendor selling ads for the paper she worked for, *The Potpourri*. I watched in amazement as she fearlessly door-knocked all the Santa Clara fairground booths—trying to get new customers. The flea market is a tough crowd to sell to, and I watched as she developed a skill that improved authentic-based sales. She moved up quickly in the company due to her fearlessness in sales and was put in charge of corporate accounts—the top salesperson at her office. She and my dad would fly yearly to different exotic locations to attend the awards ceremonies for the best of the best. She went from selling twenty-dollar ads to handling the company's most significant accounts. I was proud of her success. My mom is the kindest person I know, and she showed me that sales aren't about being shticky or rude—more is accomplished with kindness and tenacity.

That kindness came from my mom's dad. He was a World War II vet in the Air Force who flew over thirty missions as a B-24 waist gunner—earning the Distinguished Flying Cross. He casually told me stories of shooting down planes and narrowly escaping death when he bent down to pick something up and a bullet flew above his head. Although a war hero and great competitive athlete, Kenneth Diehl was the kindest man I had ever known—who happened to raise my mom.

Grandpa "D," as I called him, showed me love and support and taught me to be present and supportive. Growing up on Tonawanda Street in Buffalo, New York, he didn't have an easy life, but he never talked of hardship in his childhood or the war. He never spoke negatively of anybody, either. I spent a lot of time with him, and he gave me the safety and security and stability I needed, especially from a male role model. We would go to the Bay Meadows horse racetrack, play catch, watch the Buffalo Bills and Oakland A's, and swim a lot. He had a 1970s La-Z-Boy chair he would rock in and carve apple slices to look like little boats, as we'd sit and watch horse racing or baseball and share the apple pieces. Sharing a piece of fruit while he rocked in his chair brought peace that I still carry when sharing food with my kids. It was simple and loving. I loved being there, away from my life of intensity. I believe that this loving mentality, the peaceful soldier personality, created a good portion of what became my parenting connection. My grandfather gave me that stable love when my life was anything but that. He guided me with a paternal energy that I carry to this day.

My parents were working relentlessly hard at their jobs. My dad got his real estate license at thirty-seven, after working odd jobs for the last few years since the shop closed. He worked at the Cornish & Carey office—now the eBay campus in San Jose—and was consistently on the board for salesperson of the month. Nothing is given in real estate, and nothing happens if you don't get clients. Meaning it's all self-driven. There are slim to no company-created leads, so self-initiative is a requirement.

Both of my parents were now in sales, doing well, and for the first time, we started gaining some financial momentum. After a quick house hunt, they found a 4500-square-foot monster house in one of the most exclusive parts of Los Gatos with views of San Francisco. It was a foreclosure, and the contractor had fallen on hard times. He was living in the house and stealing power from the neighbor with a 100-foot electrical cord. He cooked out of the fireplace, and large smoke stains went ten feet up the incredibly high walls. Some doors off the dining room and living room led to two-story drops to nowhere—except the unfinished concrete patio foundation below with large rebar rods sticking out. This house was perfect.

NHL players, NFL players, and even Steve Wozniak, the cofounder of Apple Computers, lived on our street. There were optometrists, dry cleaning moguls, and artists. I started feeling a sense of pride. We were living among greatness—people who reached the highest level in their field. I never knew normal. I went from the trailer to the mansion. This rebel family had arrived with our orange van still repping in the driveway—a wonderful reminder of the crazy journey.

One morning in 1991, I woke to an unbearable stomachache and couldn't eat breakfast. My fever was 103, so my parents and I went to the doctor, who brushed it off as the stomach flu. That night, though, I saw the look of panic in my mom's eyes when she looked at the thermometer, which read 105 degrees Fahrenheit. Minutes later, we were in the hospital emergency room, where they said I had appendicitis and my appendix had ruptured. After a quick explanation, I said goodbye to my crying parents and the doctors rolled me into emergency surgery. Being wheeled alone through those operating room doors surrounded by adult strangers in sterile outfits was intimidating.

When I awoke in the recovery room, my parents were beside me, and I was more talkative than usual. I spent a week in the hospital. I remember that a few friends came from school, but many didn't. One friend, named Joe Moses, came multiple times and walked the hallways with me while I carried my IV pole and had tubes still hanging out of my side to collect the extra fluids. Moses was the kind of kid that everyone knew. He gave off an energy like he was the mayor, seemingly always doing well and living a good, stable life. He also had a large family with brothers and a sister. This was in direct contrast to my life. There was something in those walks, though, that felt like we would be friends for a long time. Moses didn't seem like he was forced to be there; it was like he wanted to be, and he was present in our conversations while we walked those halls. He was the connection to a peer that I needed.

Whatever medicine they gave me put me into a different world of happiness. The nurses would come in every few hours and give me another dose in the leg. I had a button I would press for more medicine, even though, honestly, it became more for the thrill than the pain. In my final plunge into the happy land, they stuck my leg as usual but somehow hit a nerve, and it permanently took away the feeling in my upper thigh. To this day, I have little feeling in my upper leg. I didn't realize this was a powerful drug, morphine, and I was getting quickly addicted to it—my first experience with drugs.

After a few months, I was fully recovered except for a few lingering stomach issues and trips to the ER for intestinal blockage. I wasn't sure what could happen next, but at this point, I didn't care too much. It was one of the best years of music ever. The artists I discovered were speaking their truths of pain and struggle, just what I needed.

I remember going with my mom to the Wherehouse music store, where I bought the last tape I ever purchased.

I pulled Naughty by Nature's debut album off the shelf in its large plastic anti-theft case. The cover with its parental advisory sticker and the lead singer, Treach, holding a machete sold me. This album changed my artistic world. It contained "Everything's Gonna Be Alright." "O.P.P." was good, but "Everything's Gonna Be Alright" was the most honest tune I had ever heard. It merged all the elements I liked in music—honesty, grit, quick lyrics, and raw as hell. This song wasn't fluffing it up with all the creative abstract concepts. Treach talked very honestly about how awful his young life was.

"Everything's Gonna Be Alright" spoke to all my emotions I'd had since I was five years old, and I connected with the lyrics 100 percent. The song about living with little hope was dark, heavy, and lyrically complex. Treach had a skill unlike anyone else who had ever touched the mic—not just in my opinion. I wasn't from the hood and barely ever fought—at that time. But I had lost everything twice, lived in a trailer, and almost died. I was becoming a teenager and finally found something connected with how I felt.

Then Kurt Cobain changed music by not being confined to a single genre. He flipped the heavy metal, big-hair, leather-jacket vibe of the 1980s on its head. Nirvana's music had inner angst and sadness that tapped into the experience of so many of us. Nirvana was the suburban kid equivalent to Naughty by Nature. I think many of us haven't forgotten the first time we saw the "Smells Like Teen Spirit" music video on MTV. It was so fresh and new. It was unintentionally telling us what was cool. From that moment forward, what was cool had changed. Over-the-top music was replaced with this new genre. It was so melancholy and dark, but a bit of Beatles pop simultaneously. It was the rebels' answer to what the generation before was listening to. I spent countless hours channeling the authentic delivery Kurt Cobain sang with. It was edgy. It felt like he might snap at any moment—floating between extraordinarily soft and vulnerable to enraged. The emotional rollercoaster these lyrics contained made a tremendous impact on me.

I now had all the elements to build my style. The high-pitched grit of Axl Rose, the flow and lyrical honesty of Treach, and Kurt's vulnerable, emotional rollercoaster formed my vocal style. I listened to many other artists and groups, but these three individuals stood out to me. You can hear the hybrid of early influences in my voice, subconsciously picking up pieces of these musical geniuses. I would use them as mentors. I didn't just listen to the music. I took listening to the songs as a masterclass, rewinding the music hundreds of times to make sure I got down all the aspects of the delivery—not to imitate, but to pick up on the highest levels of authenticity in delivery.

The opposite is what real life presented me. As I entered eighth grade, I was presented with the most inauthentic expression of music—cheeseball school musicals didn't fit within my self-taught musical masterclasses. I was looking to Kurt, Axl, and Treach for inspiration. I didn't fit within sterile, non-entertaining musical numbers from a Catholic school—too many parents want PG-rated lives for their kids. Daily life seems to be more R-rated. I don't think we go through life or our days at the PG level, so why do we pretend to expose our kids to a PG world? They, as well as we, know it is more complex than that.

I was standing on the back pew of the stage in the gym, practicing for the school musical, *Grease*, and I couldn't get out of my head how out of touch with actual art and music it was. In my youthful opinion, our music teacher and the participants gave it no creative expression and it was forced, robotic, and ridiculously boring. I couldn't stand the fake smile song and dance shit. I raised my hand in the middle of class while standing on the back pew. I said to the teacher, "Is this musical mandatory?" The teacher said no, so I not-so-respectfully got off the bench and said I would not participate.

I was ready to step into my rebellious nature. The time had arrived to break from the usual path and go my own way. I needed this moment. It felt great to have a little bit of control in my life.

I watched from the audience for the next month as the rest of the class rehearsed. I sat surrounded by empty chairs. I was happy to defend true art and reject the hatchet job they were creating. The school tried to make me feel regretful about my decision. Glares and scowls were on most teachers' faces. A few "I can't believe you are doing this" comments were said. I didn't care. I was expressing myself and taking a stand. The music teacher gave me an "F" for not participating in the performance. Yeah, she lied about it not being mandatory—but I didn't care. Music meant too much to me.

Finding Purpose Through Pain

Embrace the climb back out of the trenches of despair. Find pride when you make it to new heights. Don't let those from your past bring you down or make you feel bad for your progress—it is well-earned and deserved. When my parents bought our large house overlooking Silicon Valley, some tried to diminish our success by either focusing on our past struggles to dismiss our arrival or declaring we had changed. I learned the value of standing proud in the face of judgment. Some will make you feel almost ashamed of your success. That's one of the biggest red flags—and it's when both friends and foes reveal themselves.

The act of bouncing back in life carries a tremendous sense of accomplishment, but it's also important to recognize that this moment can be temporary. When the mentality is forward-looking, regardless, then the highs and lows are just a by-product of life.

Refusing to deviate from your fundamental principles is vital. Establishing moral boundaries and taking charge of your path gives a sense of freedom that no one can take away. When I stood on the stage during practice for the school musical and asked if participation was mandatory, I was choosing authenticity over acceptance—my first major moment of rebellion and independence. You need reminders sometimes as to who's in control—you are. You are the one steering the wheel on this journey.

Embrace the inner rebel. Own the road ahead.

CHAPTER 5

NO NEED FOR ALARM

On my birthday, two months into my first year of high school, a Pearl Valencia drum set awaited me in my room. I loved it. It was old, and my dad repainted the faded parts of the trim. I identified as a musician and drummer, and now I'd be able to say I had an actual drum set, not just a little drum pad. As I continued forming my identity, I was a sponge for picking up different hobbies within the lifestyle of the misfits.

Northern California in the mid-1990s was the golden era for board sports. It was the beginning of snowboarding in Lake Tahoe. Up until that time, snowboards weren't even allowed at many ski resorts. Big No Snowboarding signs graced the sides of the lodges. This kind of added to the fun in a way. It made the sport so "punk rock" or counterculture. It made us the misfits on boards. Also, surfing in Santa Cruz was becoming huge. We would go almost every weekend and play punk rock and hip-hop that helped to define the culture.

I connected with a group of friends in high school who were all about skateboarding. Some were two years older than me, and some could drive, so we would drive around San Jose, Los Gatos, and Santa Cruz to find skateboard spots. It felt so right. We constantly got kicked out of parking lots and other places with big No Skateboarding Allowed signs. For the first time in a long time, I felt like I had a culture to connect with. I would buy magazines like *Thrasher* and *Transworld Skateboarding*, trying to quickly soak up the energy of the culture and align with the attitude present in twentysomething professional skaters.

The magazines had a lot of music ads, too. Flipping through *Thrasher* magazine, I saw the ad encompassing everything the skate scene was about at the time. The cover of Del the Funky Homosapien's album, *No Need for Alarm*, was the perfect identity piece. It had graffiti, a boombox, and a parental advisory sticker. It was excellent skate music, and I felt it perfectly represented the time and the scene I was immersed in. I bought hand-me-down size 42 cutoff pants, a flannel, Airwalk shoes, a backpack, and a few skate hats. It was the first time fashion was exciting to me.

After school, I was skating in front of campus with some friends, and one friend wanted to ride my new board—I had bought it only a few days earlier. As my friend skated around, a lowered red Volkswagen bug cruised by. They circled back, pulled right before us, and jumped out. As my friend handed me my skateboard, I turned around, coming face to face with a man in his early twenties. He said, "Why you talking shit?" swung hard with a right cross, and knocked me out into the bushes. I remember lying there thinking, *What the hell just happened?* I really did see stars and was disoriented. I watched him walk away with my new skateboard, get into the car, laughing, and take off.

I got up, more embarrassed than anything, and looked around. My friends had all left the scene—getting away from danger as quickly as possible. I didn't, though. I was frozen in that instant. I just didn't have experience in what to do. As I walked back toward the campus, I saw many kids who had witnessed the whole thing. Walking up the steps, I thought getting knocked out and hit in the face didn't hurt as badly as I thought. Honestly, I felt like I just had a rite of passage. Moses, who was now going to the same high school as me, was there with us, memorized the car's license plate, and rushed into the principal's office to file the police report. However, I was uninterested in pressing charges when the police arrived. I didn't see the benefit of that. I figured if I pressed charges and these were real gangsters, which they appeared to be, that would not be a wise decision. I decided the best move would be to be prepared mentally and physically for the next time something happened.

The experience had shocked me. It came out of nowhere, and I got attacked—another danger that could happen at any time. From then on, I knew it was time to develop armor. I started lifting weights daily. I would see the red Volkswagen driving around occasionally, and instantly, fear would come over me. I thought I might get attacked. Slowly, though, I was building confidence. I was doing what I could to ensure I would be ready the next time. I couldn't prevent the random attacks, but I could reduce the inner chaos when something did happen. I could take control of my body and ensure I was ready to defend myself when the time came. I vowed not to stop and to never take more than two or three days off from physical training—that is still my mindset today, more than thirty years later.

The losses continued. I was at my dad's parents' house—running around with my cousins—when my grandfather stopped me in the front entry hallway, looked at me, and kissed me on the cheek. He had never shown me love before and never even sat to talk with me. This was not a good moment. It didn't seem loving, more of a goodbye embrace.

A few weeks later, my dad's parents sued my dad over a disagreement on a loan repayment from years earlier. All contact with my grandparents, aunts, uncles, and cousins stopped. I had known loss in many areas of life. However, experiencing a family being separated and divided over money further solidified my thoughts on the value of material things. Life is about experiences, connecting with others, accomplishments, and love—not things. Life is about family—whether blood-related or not. Life is about embracing those who support you and moving on from those who are resentful and bitter. I blame our elders for taking sides and messing up the connection for the next generation. There are lingering repercussions for the decisions of the past. There are ripple effects that permeate multiple generations for the unresolved issues and dysfunctions of previous generations.

That kiss on the cheek was the last time I saw my grandfather until I attended his funeral eight years later. It was the first time seeing all the family members together in many years. I arrived a little late and remember looking from the back of the church at his open casket sitting front and center on the altar. As I walked to the altar, I heard my cousins and family saying to each other, "Is that Ben?" It had been so long that we couldn't even recognize each other. As I went up and looked at my grandfather's face, it was just too much. I wasn't experiencing a feeling of sadness but more a lack of feeling. I had mentally moved on years before. I looked at all the family that I hadn't seen in so long, walked to the back of the church, and left. Having no contact with my extended family for almost a decade had created a void. Time didn't help fill the void where the relationship had once thrived—it just helped me forget how much they mattered. Some returned in spurts, and I'm truly grateful for that. But sadly, some things just haven't healed.

My circle of friends was quickly improving. Being an only child with a removed extended family, my peers were essential to me. One guy in particular, Frankie, stood out. He was a fearless Persian kid, constantly in Lakers purple, and would sell Cutco knives to any adult he met who had a penny to their name. He talked a lot—twice as fast as everyone else. By the time the conversation ended, you didn't know what it was about. It was like a monsoon of detailed information on meandering topics that would hit your mind at light speed. Frankie is still like that.

We would get into intense philosophical conversations and heated disagreements. Think of an Italian and a Persian in animated discussions about every possible topic imaginable. We are both stubborn and opinionated, having been through some challenging things in life. I think people can recognize others who have been through some difficult times.

I still carried the anxiety I had developed in my early trauma. Sometimes, the anxiety was more than just anxiety. I had been struggling with a sense that things were against me. That nature was out to get me. After the earthquake, I felt that this world was somewhat evil. I could almost hear the trees whistling in disapproval and taunting me when I was too still. Instead of a boogeyman lurking, the spirit of the world was that boogeyman, and he would pounce randomly—unprovoked. Events like my appendicitis, getting jumped, and losing my family further amplified that sense that something was trying to hurt me. Something out of my control was trying to bring me down. I would start to panic when I felt like I couldn't move. These were my moments of greatest anxiety—whether in the classroom, on a plane, or in a barber chair. The thought of not being able to run was terrifying. I never knew when chaos would occur. The way I coped was through my passions, the things I could get lost in. I created a world without boogeymen and sudden loss. Weightlifting and music provided me with a place of control where random evil couldn't enter. I needed to stay busy to stay comfortable. Stillness was not my friend—yet.

Finding Purpose Through Pain

You are allowed to change who you are as many times as needed until it feels right. Your identity isn't handed to you, and in the early parts of life, it is purely what you are exposed to. An identity is built through choices and reinvention. Skateboarding culture, punk music, and the rebelliousness they represented were my first chosen identity; they helped me remove the labels of my past trauma and feel alive in a way that connected to that of my motorcycle days as a youngster. You need no permission to explore and evolve.

Sometimes pain can hit without warning—violence, betrayal, heartbreak, or even just silence. You can't always stop it. But you can choose how you pivot off of it. When I got punched in the face and had my skateboard stolen, it was humiliating at first. Yet that moment pushed me into daily weightlifting, turning vulnerability into strength, embarrassment into fuel. Gain strength physically, emotionally, and spiritually—it's something you can train.

The people in your life will show you who they are when things get hard. Some will vanish, some will become foes, and some will stand firm by your side. Pay attention to this movement. Family isn't always blood—it's who shows up, who stays, and who holds you up in your weakest moments.

If your world feels hostile, dark, or unpredictable, that is not in your head. Many of us feel that. Some of us were trained by trauma. It can take years of work to feel safe in stillness. Stay in pursuit of what works for you. Time will heal if effort is present.

Finally, protect what gives you peace as if your life depends on it. These are not hobbies—they are your source of strength. Build them and keep them sharp. They are sacred, and nothing can invade this space.

CHAPTER 6

ALL EYEZ ON ME

DRIVING DOWN LEIGH AVENUE in San Jose, I saw the most fantastic car I had ever seen. It was a 1965 Chevy Malibu. I had known of the Malibu because Moses's brother had a 1964 Malibu, and we would borrow it to go skating. It had windows that rolled all the way down with no bar between the front and rear windows, and the seats were shorter, so it had an open feeling. Malibus are a hybrid, not quite a cruiser like an Impala, and not a hot rod like the Chevy Camaro—somewhere in between.

This Malibu on the side of the road hadn't moved in years, sitting underneath piles of fallen debris from the tree above. It was blue, and it looked like the owner had tried to push it toward a gangster look. It had tinted windows with the film peeling off and sat low on air shocks. I asked my mom—who was driving—to pull over, and I put a note on the car. It read: "If you want to sell, please call." Months went by, and nothing. I figured it was a dead deal.

Then came the call from the owner saying he was ready to get rid of the car. It didn't run, and just about everything was shot on it. We agreed on $800, and I didn't care about minor details like whether it ran. I got my car. My pops and I worked on the car every weekend for the next year.

We picked up a used 350 small block engine and transmission from a pick-and-pull yard a family friend owned and installed it ourselves, slowly going through most other mechanical elements before it was road-ready. Then came the time for the stereo. I had always dreamed of an Alpine. The local Circuit City had a display model, Alpine CDE-7826, for sale—a mandatory purchase. I installed it myself and wired in some 6 x 9 speakers in the rear and 6½-inch Polks in the front. This was the finalization of my mobile musical masterpiece. The car was loud with its 350 engine, headers, and Flowmaster exhaust. Of course, the music had to be even louder to be heard over the motor—mission accomplished.

My car was another example of making something from the broken. I loved to look at something broken or wounded and dream of improving it. Like the traumatized redwoods years earlier or our large house on a hill, taking the wounded and making it great was in my soul—it was me. I gravitated to the wounded and those who had potential. I surrounded myself with those who could go either way in life but had more potential than face value would show.

At age seventeen, I went to a psychiatrist. I was not doing well in school, focusing more on my social life, music, car, and weightlifting—floating between a B- and C+ average. My parents had heard of a new generation of drugs helping people concentrate. The doctor asked me if I had trouble concentrating in school. I said yes. I knew nothing about prescription pills and thought it wouldn't hurt to try them. I still had anxiety, and 2Pac's "All Eyez on Me" was my soundtrack for the good and bad feelings I was experiencing. 2Pac sang in a range of emotional honesty that went from extreme confidence to full vulnerability. I consistently would float between feelings of being the most extraordinary person in the room and the insecure little boy of the van and trailer days. The classroom was my kryptonite. It was the place of my first panic attack, and I still held the fear that everyone was watching and judging—the visions of heavy disapproval lurking in the random kid's mind. I had trouble concentrating because I felt I didn't belong, which was deeply ingrained.

I figured these pills had the potential to work magic. They had a mysterious new nature to them. The doctor said they were cutting-edge and completely safe. This visit to the doctor was my introduction to the world of drugs—courtesy of Effexor.

For the first two weeks, life was a hazy existence. I was walking around like a half zombie. I felt no anxiety, but I felt no joy either. It was a parallel-type universe with the filters of caution removed. I would raise my hand and tell jokes in class like I was sitting in my living room with good friends. Things seemed less scary—until I was late for a dose.

If I spent the night at a friend's house and forgot the medicine, I would feel distorted artificial electrical surges racing through my mind. Anxiety went through the roof, and the world seemed dark. Darker than ever before. I feared being in a place where I couldn't get to the pills.

My creativity also went way down. I couldn't find the words in freestyle rap sessions and lost my usual drive for life. The best way to put it was that I was okay with doing nothing. I was fine sitting still. The pills numbed my true identity, they were a Band-Aid in place of actually working on healing. I lost myself in an attempt to be what I was not. Instead of loving myself and embracing who I was, I tried to change to what I thought I should be.

I got off Effexor a few months later. I got off rather quickly since I didn't know the consequences and dismissed the warnings as exaggerations. My first experience with the electrical-like chills throughout the body only intensified with the long-term withdrawal and the darkness it presented. I'm not a depressed guy, but within the two weeks of getting off Effexor, I felt depressed and alone.

The kids I rolled with tended to have anger issues. A good portion of my friends were dealing with unresolved traumas. We were becoming men, gaining strength, and had hair-trigger personalities that could break out in chaos at any moment. The disorder was familiar to me. I wasn't comfortable in it, but it felt normal. I wasn't a thief, fighter, gangster, or druggie, and I didn't have suicidal ideations—but many around me did. These titles were the by-product of the disenfranchised and came with the territory of the frustrated, unfocused youth.

I had friends who were on a focused path. They participated in multiple sports and excelled academically. I also had friends who did precisely the opposite. I teetered somewhere in the middle during this time. I connected with both. I had a duality of friend groups that didn't blend. I could have gone either way if it weren't for my focus on my budding passions. As my connection to music and fitness grew, I became increasingly out of touch with where my edgier friends were headed. I was comfortable in the mental space of those with trauma, but the physical manifestations of heavy drugs, violence, and theft were not me. I watched as most of my friends either got kicked out of or left high school. As they scattered, I stayed. But I didn't feel grounded. I was floating between two worlds—one foot in survival, the other in something I still couldn't name. Something that looked like growth.

I will never forget a friend telling me I was ultra "straight edge," then dying of a drug overdose within a year. It stuck with me how close to a dangerous path I was. We were all dealing with inner demons. Another tried to kill himself in front of me—twice. These were manifestations of those of us who were young without coping tools for our inner mind wars.

As my life in high school closed, I was full of ever-increasing confidence in my future success. I was filled with hopes and dreams as my friends all went different ways to college, and the next phase of life began.

Finding Purpose Through Pain

You may carry scars, damage, or a history of being overlooked, but none of that cancels out your potential. Restoration of cars is a beautiful thing, just like with people. You can rebuild yourself, a motor, or a home and make it something more powerful than before. Sometimes, the dismissed or broken-down have the most potential and the loudest voice waiting inside for permission to come out. Give yourself that permission.

Be wary of solutions that trade your spirit and inner drive for stability. When I first took prescription pills, it dulled my anxiety, but it also dulled my joy, creativity, and sense of identity. Numbing pain can numb your true self. The world has plenty of shortcuts that dull your edges and help make you function better within society's framework. Reject that which silences your voice, your creativity, or doesn't aid in healing or progress.

The line between progress and collapse can be razor thin. You might be surrounded by people heading in all types of different directions—some preparing for greatness and others heading toward an early demise. I had friends who dropped out, turned to violence, and died of drug overdoses. Then I had others who thrived academically and athletically. Choose your group wisely and don't follow blindly. You are not here to follow or fade away. You are here to create, to feel, to drive forward with a full throttle engine, and to always rebuild when broken.

CHAPTER 7

GOOD TIMES

Feeling kinda funky I am tripping, getting money.
When I hit up the scene, I'm always looking for the green.

"First Written Rhyme"

IN LATE 1997, WHILE attending San Jose State University, I made my first song—if you can call it that—over an instrumental on a CD by the rap group WC and the Maad Circle. Back then, CD "singles" used to be sold with two songs on them and included the instrumental of the songs to add value and justify paying for just two songs.

These "singles" were great when there was no other access to instrumental hip-hop music to rhyme over. I played the CD, ran it through my Roland KC-500 mixer/amp, plugged in my mic, and recorded it to a tape deck. In a way, I guess this was my first recording studio. I wrote the first lyrics since the "Apple Juice with Leaves" tune over a decade prior using this setup.

I continued writing music from there. I would make drumbeats on my Yamaha DTX digital drum kit, then overdub back and forth between tape decks to make a song layer by layer. I left a tape of some music I was working on in a friend's car—intentionally testing if there would be a response. He left me a voicemail: "Shit, Ben! I had no idea you could flow like that. You kept it all to yourself." Through these little glimpses, people got into my world, and I began to gain confidence in my lyrical ability. People had heard my freestyles, but putting them on tape made it permanent. Now I needed some help getting my music out there, as I wasn't yet confident enough to do that myself.

I was driving home from Gold's Gym in Campbell with a friend after hitting some new personal records—feeling very confident —when he said, "I know someone stronger than you."

To me, this was an interesting statement. I had now been lifting every day for six years, and if people weren't on steroids or collegiate football linemen, I could outlift them. Not asking any more questions and always loving a challenge, I said, "Set up a lift-off!"

When Brian Hennessy and I met at Gold's Gym, we went to work—blasting through a chest workout that tested our character and integrity. We pushed on with every ounce of effort in our bodies with friends monitoring forms and reps. Neither of us wanted to lose on any sets—everything mattered. We battled and entered the dark place of the mind that only the most extreme levels of physical exertion take you. In the end, I was stronger by the smallest of margins. One repetition of difference separated these two young men willing to go through a living hell. We were willing and ready to take life to extremes. We started lifting every day together from then on—both wanting to be challenged to our potential.

We hammered at whatever we did. We challenged each other to get stronger, called each other out, and positively influenced each other's lives. We started a gardening business, and Hennessy bought a truck called "Big Time." We made some side money. His courage and ability to outwork most people was infectious and crucial to helping me push forward. I saw him killing it in college with a double major while juggling work and fitness. Slowly, we were gathering a crew with our high energy and confidence.

Hennessy and I were at a party at Santa Clara University when we decided to split up to meet new people, and we would circle back at the end of the night. Walking around the party solo, I stumbled into a girl I had gone to high school with, Angela. She was pretty, Sicilian and Hawaiian, and I remembered having a few classes at my high school with her. As we stood there on the porch, time stood still. We talked with the ease of already knowing each other. It was so comfortable. When we looked up, the party had ended, and everyone had left—we were still standing there.

This connection was different. Angela was different. We returned to her dorm room and looked up our astrology signs to see if they matched—it turned out they did. She was worldly, and her dorm room had pictures of her travels. From that night forward, she treated me like a king, making me morning cinnamon rolls in the community kitchen. I would leave in the morning, jumping in my Malibu filled with the comfort I hadn't known. She could be intense with her Sicilian-filled energy and calm and passionate within a few minutes—as I was. We could just as easily steal the college security golf cart and drive it around in the grass at 2:00 a.m. as we could take a walk on the beach after having lunch in Monterey. But most importantly, she seemed to get me. There was a familiarity within a short time that shouldn't allow that feeling—and that scared me.

We'd only been dating a few months when she told me she was heading to Washington, DC, for the summer.

The moment she said it, something in me recoiled—an old wound opened, one I hadn't fully acknowledged. I wasn't prepared to lose someone who, in such a short time, had come to mean so much. Instead of facing the fear, I shut down. Not because I didn't care, but because I cared too much. I buried my feelings, convinced myself I didn't need her, when the truth was, I didn't know how to hold on without getting hurt. I wasn't secure enough for a long-distance relationship, so I let her go mentally before she had the chance to leave me physically.

Angela left for Washington, and my grandparents and parents settled their dispute out of court. I kept picturing my father looking over at his parents in a courtroom, and I can't imagine the hurt and lack of love that he felt looking into the eyes of his own parents. We put our glorious home on the market to pay for the settlement agreement—our time in the mansion in the hills had concluded. This marked the end of my teenage years, and I was about to enter a new phase in life as I transitioned into my twenties.

We then returned to the property that started it all, in the Santa Cruz Mountains, where we had lost our home twice. We moved back into the place of all the trauma. It was difficult as I went to college and returned to this property that held so many confused and unresolved feelings. Life brought me back to the place of so much pain and confusion—for the third time. I kept returning to the land of the burnt redwoods. Now they were much larger—but still carrying the scars.

I started having a dream that would continue throughout my life. It involved a house and me going inside and needing to enter a basement. The basement would have countless flights of stairs, and the evil energy would increase as I went deeper into the abyss. I would eventually be at a dungeon level, standing before a sizeable boarded-up door with pure evil lurking behind it. I would never open it. Every time I have this dream, I awaken in panic at this door. I was at the home of the fear that had tormented me most of my life. I was returning to the place of the original pain. I had a long way to go to harness the flames.

Since our second year of high school, 4 Finger Pete and I had been friends. He got his name from being a bass player, and we always jammed with him on various guitars and me on drums. We officially became a band in my parents' garage—a room removed from the dining room table where I wrote the apple juice song. He brought over a new Roland VS-840 digital 8-track recorder, and the songs poured out as quickly as we could hit the RECORD button. I laid down a drum track with the DTX, and he asked me to get on the mic for the verse. I then went "into the studio" for the first time. When he pressed RECORD and I heard the intro guitar, I felt like my whole life's musical and personal journey was about to be let out. I could feel my emotions about to pour out from my soul. I was like a racehorse being let out of the gate. I felt at home.

> *Time to get in the car and go for a trip, go down to the water and take a dip, hang out with the boys from S.I.P. . . .*
>
> *"Good Times"*

I was finally able to get out the power that I felt inside. Weightlifting could physically relax the inner angst, but music could release the soul's torment. This was no music ready for airplay, but it did contain something—a spark of uniqueness I was proud of. I gave a tape to a few friends to listen to and wasn't sure what they would think—all I knew was I liked it.

Hennessy called me while I was standing on my parents' back porch. He said he had played the tape of my music at a house party, and people liked it. When I went to a party at the school a few days later, people came up to me telling me how good my music was. Hennessy would promote my music around the Santa Clara University campus and help me push music forward with belief in my talent—even buying me a CD recorder. We officially opened Benny B Records LLC, got a logo—Cuban link chains with a medallion made with our Double B—and I started doing open mics and small shows.

I bought a Roland VS-880 digital recorder, an MC-505 beatbox, a Joe Meek pre-amp, and a Shure KSM32 mic. I would constantly be recording. I never wanted to stop. I wanted to learn every aspect of music recording and mixing—to do it all myself. I thought of the recording and the mixing process as all part of the artistic expression, and the more I knew about that side of music, the more I could paint the musical pictures I wanted. So, a few months later, I attended Ex'pression College in Emeryville to earn a sound engineering degree.

At school, I felt a sense of belonging. This environment reminded me of my early childhood. This was the closest to a relatable tribe I had been in since the motorcycle shop days. Everyone was an artist and seemed to live by their own rules. The misfit was embraced at this school, and everyone had a personality. I felt such joy in this environment. Most days, people would come to my apartment after class, and we would work on music. I felt no anxiety because I was being true to myself—on my path to a career in music. I would wake up, lift at the Gold's Gym by Lake Merritt, spend my days in class and my nights making music. My days were focused on what I loved doing. I was living my dream. Life seemed so perfect that it scared me.

Finding Purpose Through Pain

You can start with an army of one—that is enough to begin with. When I first started recording music alone, overdubbing between tape decks layer by layer in my bedroom, I wasn't sure if anyone would listen. Don't look for the applause and support; that will come later. Start with your inner fire, your passion for that which you do. If you stay at it, then others will come and join. Your energy will attract like-minded people, and through focus and growth, it will attract the right people.

In reality, it only takes one. One friend who can push you to train harder, think critically, and create with more inspiration. Meeting Hennessy and battling him rep-for-rep in the gym showed me the power of having one like-minded, driven friend. It helped change my trajectory in fitness and music. If one person sees your potential when you're still learning how to believe in it yourself, even better. This will help in your trajectory.

With time, focus on surrounding yourself with people who are pursuing their own purpose. In my sound engineering school days, surrounding myself with dedicated artists boosted my creativity, motivation, and understanding that I had a long way to go as an artist. The collective momentum will strengthen you in school, work, and life. Choose a circle that mirrors where you are headed, not where you have been.

When support shows up, honor and nurture it, and the tribe will grow when you lead with your truth.

CHAPTER 8

TIME (CHANGES)

Times got myself, locked down . . . and I look around.
Feel the bust, time change, life's strange, rearrange.
"Time (Changes)"

My mom's parents came up to Oakland to see my apartment and the new life I was living, immersed in music. After visiting a local fish house, my grandfather wasn't feeling well—I went to the car with him while the rest of my family finished their meal. I tried to play him some songs in the car, but his hearing was going, and he couldn't make out the words, which frustrated him. Before my grandparents left, I told my grandfather that I had met a girl who was going to law school, and that I wanted him to meet her the next time I visited them. He smiled a giant smile and said he looked forward to meeting her.

I was getting ready for class the following week when I listened to my voicemail. My dad's voice was sad, and I knew what was ahead. My grandfather had passed away. The stability of my first twenty-one years was now gone. My grandfather had battled through over twenty years of sickness. He fought when the doctors thought he had only months to live. He was there for me and gave me the stability I needed. He did his part. His legacy of love and care was about to live on.

Only a few weeks after my grandfather passed away, my girlfriend became pregnant. We didn't know each other well, and we were both young, in school, and far away from a stable life. I knew what I wanted to do—music—but at the time, I was just starting to lay the groundwork for my future path. She was in law school and had years left before she was ready to begin her career. With her pregnancy, though, we both stepped up to the plate. We tried to balance all of the various aspects of life.

It all hit me when I packed up my apartment in Emeryville with a few friends and my mom—it felt like my youth was slipping away. When I closed the door the last time, I looked over at my mom as I locked the door. Her facial expression still lives in my mind. The pain in her eyes. The knowledge of what a difficult path I had ahead was all over her face. Only now, as a father with a son the same age as I was then, do I understand how hard this moment was for a parent. I was naïve about the brutal road ahead.

We named our son Kennedy—after my grandfather Ken, who had died only ten months before his birth. Kennedy was the sweetest kid. From day one, his demeanor was calm and kind—very similar to my grandfather's. His mom and I had different thoughts on developing a family, and these differences started to show quickly. We wanted different things out of life—different values for raising our son. As the initial infatuation faded, the reality of these two young adults coming together became obvious. We tried to keep it together in our little condo in Fremont, California, but our lifestyles were too different. The end felt so near, even as the months quickly ticked on.

I left sound engineering school and worked as a pro audio salesman at a Guitar Center to support my son. I loved being around music and all the gear I wanted so badly, but I kept thinking about the life I had left so quickly after starting up at sound school. My classmates were approaching the end of their education and about to graduate. They were about to take off into the world of entertainment. I worked long hours for low pay and had minimal time to work on music.

I did find a different talent, though—sales. On my first day, a musician approached me and said he wanted to buy a rig. Over $10,000 worth of gear later, I had made one of the most significant first-day sales that any of my coworkers had ever seen.

After my initial success, I realized that I loved talking to people. Instead of waiting for people to approach me, I went up to them and asked how I could help them when they walked through the doors to the pro audio department. Even if they said they were just looking, I would ask what type of music they were into. I loved the connection, and it wasn't about the sale as much as helping people with what they wanted to do in music. I quickly rose through the sales ranks until I hit the ranking of top salesperson for the month. It seemed all the years of watching my mom sell had paid off. Compared to flea market sales, this was relatively easy. Potential customers were entering my place of business, so I knew they were interested in what we sold.

I tried all the mics and got good at talking to strangers about the gear as I learned about it. Also, a lot of significant musicians would roll through there. Strangely, the movie *This Is Spinal Tap* played on a TV on repeat all day, every day. One day, a guy came in, looked up at the video, and said, "That's a handsome fellow right there." Sure enough, it was David Kaff, also known as Viv Savage, the keyboardist from Spinal Tap. The store became my escape where I didn't need to think about the inevitable future that awaited me.

At our condo in Fremont, I turned the little garage into a music studio. I bought my first Pro Tools rig, the Digi001, with the money my grandfather left me when he passed away. When I fired up this workstation for the first time, the inner world of music shone brighter than ever before. I had a space unlike any I had ever known—a world inside music.

Life was chaotic outside the walls of that room. I wasn't ready to live the lifestyle of thirty- and forty-year-olds. Inside those walls, my creativity flowed endlessly. My twenty-two-year-old self could soar as high as I wanted—pun intended. I wrote alone in the late-night hours in this windowless space. I had a jug to pee in so I wouldn't be disturbed—I didn't want to leave this space for more time than needed.

The song that best defined this era of my life was "Time (Changes)," which my friends called "Thorn Tattoo." It dealt with the quick turnaround to domestic life and responsibilities after less than a year of pursuing my musical dream. Time might have had me locked down, but I was able to channel my experience through the music.

In this musical space of the garage, life was more than okay. I was working toward something. I knew I had to keep going—for my sanity. The potential of the next song burned bright. The feeling that the next song would be my best kept me constantly trying to crack the code and find greatness in a piece of art. My time in the Fremont garage was the beginning of the domestic escape in life I now live and cherish. My immersion into digital recording, mixing, and songwriting began not at school but as most other things I did in life—alone inside the music in my garage.

I needed to make more money, though. On the way home from working at Guitar Center, I used to buy luxury home magazines, and I visualized myself in these houses as I flipped through the pages. I also did the math. The commission on $10,000,000 in sales was $250,000. I wanted either music or real estate to get me there. At Guitar Center, I was selling musical gear. I had my music, so optimizing my income through the highest level of sales seemed right. It was time for a change. I got my real estate license a few months later and joined Coldwell Banker Los Gatos.

My mom had joined my father in real estate back in 1997, so our family income came only from commissions. There is no salary or money coming in if you don't have clients. The pocketbook of this feast or famine life can be brutal and unstable. You can be doing very well, only to have a dry spell that drains everything. Recessions are moments of sleepless nights and panic—if not properly prepared. So in 2003, my parents and I formed a family real estate team, called "The Barbics."

Kennedy, his mom, and I moved into a house on Saratoga Avenue and started fixing it to make it feel like a home. As we worked on painting the house, the tension just kept increasing. The darkness of our life grew. Time together was pulling us further apart, not closer together. One night, I needed to leave the house—I felt trapped and isolated. I went to the gym with my friend. At Gold's, I had a moment that still lives in a mental snapshot. I felt Kennedy and his mom leaving. I could sense that this was a moment of change. I looked out the gym window into the darkness of the night and knew my life had just shifted once again. I drove home to a house I knew would be empty.

The car was gone, and the house was silent, stripped of the energy a toddler brings. My life had officially taken a different direction. I looked around the home, and everything was left undone. The half-filled paint buckets, floors covered in plastic, and all the doors off their hinges reminded me of life's abrupt change. I knew this feeling well. I stayed in this space for the next few months—plastic still on the floor. The house remained in limbo, like me. Unsure of my next move, I just waited. Nothing changed. I was letting life get the better of me. I did have my cat Jerome, who had been with me since I was 21, and she left our cat Cameron. They got along too well to separate them. It comforted me that at least Jerome and Cameron were still with me, although my son wasn't most of the time.

I was letting life beat me down lower and lower—constantly finding a new rock bottom mentally that I had yet to experience. My drive to sell houses went into the toilet. My drive to progress at anything was now missing. I was no longer motivated to provide for a family that was no longer there. I also wasn't prepared for the void of not being around my son.

From then on, I saw my son one night every two weeks. I was deprived of spending the precious memories of early childhood with him. The first words, steps, and days of school were moments we couldn't share. Every other week, I drove two hours to pick him up at preschool, then dropped him off at a park one hour from my house. It was six-plus hours of driving for twenty-four hours with my son. I would always be wrecked, crying openly on the drive home. The next day after dropping him off, I couldn't pretend to be okay. I would hide from the world, shaken by the situation.

Sometimes I would be in open houses waiting for clients and write lyrics about my pain. I would be alone inside my hurt, and then a knock would come at the door. "Hello!"—smiling and welcoming them in was hard. I would do my best to snap out of the silence and heaviness in my mind and try to sell a home to people decades older and more successful than me. I was still driving my 1965 Malibu, now in disrepair from years of use and break-ins while living in Emeryville. I would park it around the corner because no one would buy a home from someone driving a beat-up classic car—that's what I thought. My dad did the same thing when he got into real estate and still drove the orange van. I wasn't what people expected in a realtor, and I wasn't comfortable enough to show them who I was.

I didn't care about anything. All I wanted to do was numb the pain and discomfort. I took the challenges life threw at me and thought I could overcome them, I could deal with the pain, I could ride out the misery, but I couldn't. Life knocked me the fuck out.

While going out at night, I didn't seem to care as much about outcomes. I wasn't a fight starter, but I found comfort in not taking any shit. I was entering a dangerous phase when my inner unrest was strong enough that potential repercussions didn't carry much weight in my decision-making. I spent New Year's Eve in a town I wasn't from, sat in a bar full of local patrons, and established a quick rapport with the bartender. He started pouring free shots of Everclear, clocking in at 190 proof.

After a few shots, I felt pretty loose and made friends with the patrons around me. I mentioned a few times that

I was from the Bay Area in conversation, not as a flex, but purely to share the location of a few stories I had. I got up to use the bathroom, and a giant bouncer blocked the door. He got right in my face and said, "Fuck you." I went back to my seat and sat down. I told the guy with face tattoos beside me what the bouncer had said, and he replied, "You don't wanna fuck with that guy." As I sat there, thinking of the times when I didn't stand up for myself, the memories came back to me—the skateboard incident my first year of high school—and various times I was made fun of and didn't back myself up. Now, I didn't feel like that kid anymore. I was full of pain, twenty-two years old, and three-plus shots of Everclear deep. I decided to take a stand. Since I was alone, and he knew everyone, I knew I couldn't win. That didn't matter. It was about standing up for myself because that felt like all I had left. It was the wrong day to insult me, and I made an impulsive and ill-advised decision.

I stepped outside, where the bouncer was talking to three other guys—all about 300 pounds and six feet four inches tall. I approached him and asked, "You got a cigarette?" As he walked toward me, ready to fight, I tried putting him in a chokehold. I didn't quite manage it. He and his friends had a knee on my head, pressing the side of my head into the concrete sidewalk until the cops came twenty minutes later.

Sitting in jail that night, I felt a weird sense of accomplishment having stood up for myself. I lost the fight in every way—it was pretty much unwinnable. But I refused to back down, and in that moment, my pride was all I had.

I've since taken a tremendously different approach to life. My pride is not so thin and shallow that a "fuck you" makes me risk everything. I realize now what I didn't then: Beware of being in the wrong place at the wrong time. That night was a textbook example.

I was not healing. The pain was growing inside. I was empty and kept going out, surrounding myself with others full of anger and hopelessness. Less than a month later, I was at a bar in downtown Los Gatos that a friend was bartending at. What started as just a few friends turned into a larger group, and I was all for the energy of chaos. Not only was I going through a heavy time, but I was drinking and hanging around people who were also not thriving. As my friend Nick and I were walking back to the bar, Nick saw a guy he thought he knew and said, "You from San Jose?" The man responded, "Fuck San Jose!" As he approached, it was apparent that he was going to fight. I wrapped him up in a chokehold in the bar's parking lot, but he was a good wrestler. We grappled on the asphalt, all the while I was maintaining my hold, when my glasses flew off and broke. In the most undesirable of coincidences, the cops randomly entered the parking lot. I wasn't able to really see what was happening except the lights flashing in front of me, so I released my hold, and after an explanation that didn't seem to help my case, I went back to jail for fighting—as did the other guy. The following morning, we were both released at the same time. Enemies the night before, we were now calmly waiting together to get picked up in front of the jail. We didn't even have any ill will. It was all just a release of pent-up frustration and anger—with significant repercussions.

I have a few lessons for you. First, don't get drunk around people who are also drunk if none of you care about the consequences. Bad shit will happen, and it's not even personal—it's circumstantial. Second, two people can have a negative encounter one night, and then, like magic, the next day all is forgotten. They can engage in a standard, decent conversation. Third, the reality is that two enemies probably have much more in common on any given night than they realize. Finally, you can have a case and legal matters to deal with over nothing. I risked my entire future fighting someone I had nothing against and defending someone who didn't need me to protect them. I was just at the wrong place with the wrong mindset.

I'm much different now. I don't fear a fight. But I also don't have any interest in it. If someone wants to fight, most of the time, I deny the request. I have often told people to go away when they seek confrontation. You show them you have no interest. It's like turning down a solicitation on the street to buy something. You're essentially saying, "Hello, angry person. I have no interest in accepting your invitation to hit each other in the face for no reason. Goodbye." Badass people have no time for random fights with strangers in a bar. Only insecure grown children do this. That's why I avoid dive bars like the plague—no good can come from it. I'm a reasonably big guy as of this writing—215 lbs. The last thing I want is to randomly stumble across someone in a similar place to where I was so long ago, ready to engage in nonsense. Life is too beautiful to dwell in the darkness.

I went to a psychiatrist north of San Francisco to document that I was changing my ways—I didn't want my behavior to be an issue when it came to child custody. I told him my story, watching him zero in on the fighting aspect and labeling me what could only be described as a "loose cannon." The darkness of the mental clouds that hung over me during this time led me to a very reckless decision. I would tell the doctor what I knew would get me the pills. I knew what he was. He was another Band-Aid drug dealer. He was a pill guy—giving me three prescriptions by the end of the session. Effexor, Depakote, and Strattera were now my morning and evening prescription cocktails. I left there with a strange feeling, hoping these could make me Superman. Perhaps these pills would make me fearless and ready to take on the world.

I was wrong. I felt like a walking zombie—void of emotion as my body acclimated to these potent drugs. I was becoming OK with less drive or ambition. I didn't have the same creative spark. I also didn't have feelings of much at all. In a sense, life was easier due to being stripped of the uncomfortable emotions that are part of being human. Pain, sadness, excitement, and motivation were all diminished or removed from the experience. In my moment of weakness at that doctor's office, I put myself into a tough predicament. I also didn't see any way I could get out of it.

The drugs changed my cravings as well. Instead of wanting to lift weights and make music, my body now craved more drugs. I started chewing tobacco. I also smoked ganja—every day. I put on lots of weight. Further, I had no motivation to eat right—I had been on a healthy diet most of my life as a young adult. My body's response seemed to be that I was already starting my day lost in the haze—I might as well just continue the ride.

If I missed a dose or forgot to refill my prescription, I felt like a drug addict at the pharmacy. I couldn't stop taking these pills and felt like a prisoner to my meds, but I always needed them. My days revolved around keeping the bottle close by. I remembered what it was like getting off Effexor the first time, so the thought of withdrawals from these was terrifying.

I share my experience with meds cautiously. Some people need pills—they can be a blessing. These drugs are lifesavers for millions—needed to function and enjoy life. I am grateful to the scientists who have worked to find treatments for mental illness. I'm thankful that people can enjoy a life they wouldn't otherwise. For many, there can be a balance of improved lifestyle, healthy habits, and medicine. Time and intensely personal work rid me of the intensity of my inner mind war. I wish the same for anyone struggling with mental illness or a difficult time.

If you are one of those people, I offer no judgment. Instead, I'm referring to the over-prescribed, numbed-out society we live in. Moments of mental weakness can create a lifelong pill reliance. Pills are zombifying people's potential and drive—prescription pills can take a life in motion and make it stationary, which is what happened to me.

To me, the cover of the season one *Sopranos* DVD looked cheesy. I thought this couldn't be a good mob series. I started with the first episode in the living room of the Saratoga Avenue house, surrounded by plastic-covered floors and chaos—at the peak of my unrest. As Tony Soprano's life unfolded on the screen, it felt like I was watching parts of my own of my life. The panic attacks, the prescription meds, and the need for help were all familiar. Watching a show about a mob boss in therapy helped me feel like getting help was okay. It allowed me to face the fact that I could also use some help. I needed life assistance. The fictional world was in line with my mental space. I would go to sleep with *The Sopranos* playing in the background—sweet dreams were not had. But I had something that I could relate to—something that matched the darkness I felt inside. I also, more importantly, felt like I had permission to go to therapy.

My first day in therapy felt so comfortable because of this show—as crazy as that sounds. My therapist, Dr. Elmare, was also from New Jersey, and I would watch *The Sopranos* and then have my own version of Tony Soprano's time in the office. These sessions quickly became the highlight of my week. I could be honest—mostly—and during the week would often think about what I would discuss in the next session. These sessions were personal therapeutic healing, not just a Band-Aid.

What Dr. Elmare did was make me feel OK. She put everything into perspective and made me feel like a good person who needed a tune-up. I wanted to share wins with her, and we worked through my losses. She listened and gave me support. I needed to hear that I was a good father. I needed to hear that I was a wounded but loving young man. I needed guidance that life had not given me.

Finding Purpose Through Pain

You will have distinct transitions in life. Markers that change what you have known and grown comfortable with. Dreams can become distant as life's responsibilities take precedence. When forming the next phase, success may not last. Whether that's a family, career, or the like, sometimes the foundation is not strong enough, and it all crumbles. When I packed up my Emeryville apartment, I saw the pain in my mom's eyes as she recognized the difficult road ahead—my youth fading nearly instantly as an uncertain future awaited me. This moment when things end is critical.

Without a proper personal foundation, life can go off the rails. Issues can arise legally and otherwise when the mind state is unsettled, and you are walking around with an "I don't care" attitude. If this happens, it is imperative to acknowledge the issue and fix things systematically, through everyday growth and progress. The quick fix will not work. Band-Aids won't heal the wounds. Returning to the Saratoga Avenue house after my son and his mom left, seeing the half-filled paint buckets and the doors off their hinges, reminded me how quickly life can unravel without a stable foundation. I wasn't prepared and was left in limbo. You must find something that can help guide you through the dark times and understand that it is only temporary. Even just having one thing a week you can look forward to can be enough.

CHAPTER 9

ROCK BOTTOM

Rocks at the bottom, and I start to climb up, Darkest hour of my Life . . .

"Rock Bottom"

I CALLED TO CHECK in on Kennedy, and the call didn't go through. I returned to the table at the Mexican restaurant where my friend and I had been eating dinner, feeling very alone among the people. My friend was on the phone himself. I overheard Angela on the other end of the line—he had maintained a friendship with her since college. He said, "Angela's in SF and having some people over. You want to go?" I didn't want to go. I didn't feel like doing anything at that moment. We would get up there after 10:00 p.m., and I wanted to go home and be with my darkness. Then, like a flip of a switch, hearing her voice laughing on the other end of the line brought back some feeling I hadn't felt in a while—playful, youthful fun.

We arrived in San Francisco on August 8, 2003, around 10:30 p.m. When I saw Angela, I knew our meeting again was something significant. They were already well into the party, so there were no inhibitions. At the first glimpse of her in the hallway of her apartment, I felt joy, love, and happiness that had been absent in my life. I felt the innocence and youthful energy I'd had just four years earlier. We very quickly went into her bathroom to catch up. We emerged from our private suite three hours later, well past midnight.

Angela had recently returned from living in Spain. She was twenty-four years old and living in the Marina of San Francisco. She had a great job and a thriving social life. Angela had multimillionaires trying to "wow" her with courtside Golden State Warriors seats, world-class trips, purses, and Michelin-star dinners. She was getting recognized for everything I knew she possessed when we dated. She lived the carefree life she needed to. My life was broken and sad, but she still wanted me. We needed to let each other go to appreciate each other when we reunited—but what I offered was much less than she did at the time.

We were together from that moment. I knew I couldn't let Angela go again. We fit too perfectly. She saw my potential, even when the light was the dimmest. She believed in me when I barely did. The only positive thing I had most days was seeing her. I wasn't motivated to work. I knew I would always make music, but I was so broken that I barely finished any songs in those days. I didn't believe in myself enough to put the music out. I will never forget what she told me. We were driving through the Marin Headlands, having an adventure. I wanted her to know I wasn't staying in this place of darkness. I said, with great emotion, "I'm broken right now, but I will heal again." She responded by saying simply, "I know who you are." This was no falsity. She believed in me, riding with me through the roughest patch of my life. If she was there in my lowest moment, she deserved all the benefits of life at my optimized best. If she could handle my rock bottom, then she earned the mountain top.

Shadows in Plainview was my first released project. CDs were printed, and shirts were made—4 Finger Pete and I worked on this for months. The music had an edge and a darkness that was my life. It was filled with depression and anger. I felt great releasing what I was feeling inside. I had an outlet. People in a similar state of mind related to it.

I felt bigger than life getting off the stage after the conclusion of our set at the release party. A woman in the music industry pulled me aside as I left the stage and said I was destined for fame. "You need to go solo, and you will make it," she whispered in my ear. I wasn't mentally ready to take this all on myself. I wasn't prepared to be front and center on stage with no one else around and hundreds or thousands of people staring at me. I didn't want all eyes on me. I wasn't ready to be alone on the stage. But 4 Finger wasn't in the same place I was in life. He bowed out of the band after the release show. He drove off before the party's conclusion, and I knew he'd had enough. He was going in a different direction.

The band ended just as soon as it began. I began telling myself I had missed the boat and was too old. While recording, I looked at myself in the mirror one night and thought about how I couldn't make it in music. I looked wounded and out of shape, having reached 240 pounds from poor eating habits and the pills I was on. My inner demons were too strong, and they were winning the battle. I felt defeated.

I've called my son Kennedy "Kendo" since his earliest days. I had made a friend at Ex'pression Sound Engineering school. His name was Stinkweed (Kindred McCune). Kindred was in the hardcore band Plutocracy, and one of the most intense people I ever met—gangsta lifestyle to the core. Well, Kindred treated me like gold. If he liked you, he put an "endo" at the end of your name. He called me "Bendo." So, when Kennedy was born, I loved the sound of Kendo. Kindred died in 2012 in his thirties, but a little bit of him lives on in my life with the name I call my son. As life moves on, there is such value in the small markers from the past that can live on in the present.

I dropped Kendo off at the park Sunday afternoon when I got the call I needed. Dino had gone to school with me at St. Mary's for one year—I barely knew him. His band Dredg was signed to Interscope Records, and he toured the world constantly. I would often see him at Gold's Gym when he returned from touring. I noticed he would lift like a savage—like me. He got my number from our mutual friend Joe and left me a message. He said he was ready to lift heavy when not on tour and asked if I wanted to lift with him. I needed this. To show up to the gym with a local celebrity who had people nervously going up to him as we lifted gave me a sense of pride by association. I would be with him in the gym before and after huge events. I could live elevated through affiliation. He had just played *Jimmy Kimmel Live!* a few weeks before we started lifting and was at the peak of his rock star status. I felt almost like a bodyguard to this bona fide rock star.

Dino was living a dream. I was living a nightmare. But I did have a growing list of people who mattered in my life. People who helped me through the dark times. I struggled because Dino had no interest in connecting musically at the time. But I also knew I hadn't put in the time yet. He had devoted himself to music his whole life. I was just entering the phase of everyday music creation, and albums like *Shadows in Plainview* were not ready for major labels and radio play.

During our lifting sessions, I channeled my frustrations to the next level of strength. I pushed to an insane new max. Sets with 120-pound dumbbells on shoulder presses and 150-pounders on flat bench presses were my peak. I called it "playing with the dusties" since other people rarely picked up those weights, and they were covered in dust. My main outlet was this combination of my rock star brethren and high-level strength. I wasn't yet at a comparable level in music, and no matter how difficult my days were, the gym's intensity helped me get through. Lifting with Dino came about when I needed it most, and I hadn't even hit rock bottom yet.

Nothing could have prepared me for life's next challenge. I remember playing in the yard with Kendo, who was now four. I saw that his lips were turning slightly blue. Angela and I looked at each other in confusion, and fear swept over me. After he stopped running around, the blue tint went away, and all of us knew something was really wrong.

Within a week, Kendo's mom and I sat in a windowless conference room at a long table in a heart surgeon's office.

We were told our son had a hole in his heart. The doctor explained that we had two options: perform surgery or leave things as they were. He explained the highly complex heart surgery and the healing process. He also went into the details of what would happen if we did nothing. The surgeon explained that Kendo would run into "problems" in his early twenties if the surgery wasn't performed. We set the surgery date at that meeting. The anxiety-filled countdown began.

As they wheeled him through the door to surgery, the unknown of my son's future was so heavy. I flashed on myself being wheeled through the operating room doors when I was young. I also felt the helplessness of a parent with no control over the outcome. It was in the doctor's hands—and God's. I went to the empty hospital chapel and prayed in a moment where faith was all I had. All I could do was reach out to the universe and pray for my son's life.

My prayer was answered, and the surgeon and his team were my angels. After surgery, I walked into the hospital's intensive care ward and sat beside my son, and he smiled. Within a few hours, his mom's family and mine surrounded him in the intensive care pediatric ward as he began his recovery. We stayed with him for a few days. This was the only time we were all together, and that was beautiful to experience.

Over the next two years, I was in a state of limbo. Life was a blur of uneventful moments when I wasn't with Angela and my son. I was just not motivated to push forward and didn't have the confidence to do so. I was quickly getting further off the path of life the rest of my friends were on. Life was passing me by. I started feeling bitterness and regret.

I was about to turn twenty-eight. Most of my friends were now married, had homes, college degrees, families, dogs, and promising careers. I was unhappy and had just celebrated my birthday with Angela and my son. They gave me a teddy bear that said, "We love you, Daddy," in their voices when you touched its paw, and I knew they did—but that didn't give me enough strength to save myself from a downward path. On my birthday, I was sitting at home alone in my apartment before going out with a few friends. Something didn't feel right about the night, but I ignored my intuition.

After a night at a bar I barely remember, I regretfully decided to drive home. After safely leaving the highway, I took the back way to my house. I relaxed in the comfort of the windy road I knew so well.

Boom! I slammed sideways into a pole. I sat there stunned for a minute, then gathered myself to continue the drive. Just before turning onto my street, I was startled by the lights of a cop car behind me. I pulled onto my road—mere feet from my house—and stopped. He came to my window and said my taillight was out. I didn't fight it. He knew I had been drinking, and I didn't try to lie. I gave in to the situation. On the way to the jail, handcuffed in the backseat of the sheriff's SUV, I felt myself physically surrender to the process. I didn't want to play this game anymore.

They put my body type down as obese as I was getting booked. I was now getting close to thirty years old, in a place I had been to multiple times before. The man handcuffed to the chair next to me started talking about a night in jail as if this was the local coffeehouse—he thought we were the same. I heard a familiar voice and looked up to see a friend from childhood who was a corrections officer. We pretended we didn't know each other—given the circumstances, I couldn't look him in the eye. The following day, I was released and called a friend to pick me up. Watching the sunrise, I felt a darkness I never thought I'd face. It was a silent ride home with my friend until I got out, muttering a few words of thanks. I went into my bedroom and looked at the stuffed animal my son and girlfriend had given me a few days before. I touched the little teddy bear's paw, and it said, "We love you, Daddy" in their voices. I fell to the floor and wept loudly in agony at what I had become. The example I set for my son was gut-wrenching, and I couldn't handle the pain I felt. I knew so much was ahead legally. So much was needed to climb out of this massive hole I was in. The time of change was upon me. I was done getting engulfed by the flames of life. It was time to harness the power of fire. It was time to stand tall like the ash-covered redwoods that surrounded me. It was time to rise from the ashes.

Finding Purpose Through Pain

There may come a time when life slams the brakes on everything and demands you notice. You are forced to look at what you have become, not who you are.

You might be surrounded by people who love you, but you feel unworthy of that love. When that love, that genuine care for you, even in your lowest moments, shines through, that is when the life-changing decision is upon you. That is when all the shame, regret, and embarrassment need to be turned into fuel for progress. That is when you decide that what you have become will not take you where you are going next. My son's and Angela's voices saying "We love you, Daddy" as I squeezed the teddy bear was the moment I knew what I needed to become. There was no time to waste. I could either flip the switch and thrive in the light, or I could continue to dim in the darkness.

Regrets and excuses are useless. Fuel your movement forward with what you refuse to be and stop hiding. Rise from the wreckage you have created and step into the life that is waiting for you.

It's this simple. Pain can bury you or it can build you. Make this the moment that builds you. Make this the start of your own Rise and Climb.

CHAPTER 10

EFFECTED BY THE CURE

Effected by the cure again. Orange bottle I depend. Costs a lot like troubled friends. Pills took my drive again . . .

"Effected by the Cure"

THE LONG JOURNEY UPWARD began with me paying for my mistakes. I cleaned highways for about a month—Monday to Friday. The other small-time offenders and I would pile in the vans early in the morning and spend the day on the side of the road, picking up the trash and cutting the grass and shrubs. As I worked with the crew, I learned most of their stories. There were lots of DUIs—there was a DJ, a jazz musician, and one guy who drove his date home in the morning before the alcohol had worn off. Another guy got caught driving a Hummer over 100 miles per hour in the fast lane with a trailer bumping around behind him.

Some homeless camps off the highways were disgusting, littered with trash and even shit. I stepped in some and unknowingly got human poop all over my clothes. The guy overseeing us freaked out and immediately took me back to the headquarters and gave me a white jumpsuit to wear the rest of the day. Some camps were occupied by people with jobs who couldn't afford the high rent. Some used power from the streetlight electrical lines, and one guy even had a TV—he also had an area with hangers and a makeshift closet for his work clothes.

This mandatory work was a proper place to start thinking about how I would rebuild my life. It was a moment to step out of my world and gain a new appreciation for what I had. After finishing the work program, I was required to go to substance abuse classes and group meetings—learning the dark side of alcohol. I heard story after story of people who were "unlucky." If there is one thing to take away, it's that anyone can have an unlucky moment. Moms in the car with their kids after a day at the community pool get DUIs and child endangerment charges. People driving from their friend's house, four houses down from theirs, get DUIs. There is no face, age, or profile to recklessness. Anyone can have their life turned upside down—thinking that it wouldn't happen to someone like them. People don't realize how easily things can go south. One taillight can turn into jail. Just because you're only going down the road to your house has no bearing on the potential risk. I no longer take such careless risks.

It was time to shed my dead branches. It was time to remove all of the dead weight I carried. Redwoods drop their dead branches as they grow. You can hear the limbs falling when you are among them. They are usually leafless and quite large. They come crashing down and sometimes violently pierce the ground like spears being hurled to the earth. I had many branches that needed to be removed—they were only stunting my growth.

First, I gave up alcohol and "going out." I also reduced my friend list to those with whom I did positive things. I no longer had time to kick it. I needed to focus purely on growth and trimming away that which prevented it. One by one, my dead branches fell.

I had been chewing tobacco for a few years, and Angela started putting pictures of removed cancerous jaws in my car—sick of my spit cans and nasty habit. Impressed by her care and love, I switched to Nicorette gum for a few weeks and then kicked the habit—further reducing the crutches and vices.

"Do you need to be on these meds? They are really powerful." Those words by Angela held me accountable once again. I told her I didn't—it was time to get off them. I decided to wean off in a specific order—Depakote, Strattera, and finally Effexor. This took me a few months, and I discovered how dangerous those pills were. I knew my mind would play tricks on me while I was in withdrawal. What I felt, though, was unimaginable despair—I just wanted to get out of my head. There was no escaping the discomfort—it was around every turn. It was as if my brain had been hijacked and was trying to sabotage itself. I remember driving up to San Francisco mid-withdrawal and being on the freeway overpass near the Bay Bridge, thinking I couldn't handle the feeling I was having. It was such despair that my own mind felt like a psychedelic horror movie. I didn't know my own thoughts—I was scared.

To cope, I started to visualize life after the madness of this moment, to reassure myself that this was temporary. I pictured life when I was no longer a prisoner in my mind. Soon, I would be free of the torment of withdrawal. I shifted through brain surges, intense fear, and hopelessness. Slowly, over the coming weeks, I started gaining clarity. I started having energy and enthusiasm for life.

Life wasn't all roses and sunshine. Anxiety came back, and my senses became drastically elevated. I would best explain it as feeling naked. My mind felt vulnerable and insecure. It took a while to be okay with the plethora of emotions. Most importantly, though, I felt like Ben again.

My music started to change to hope instead of despair for the first time since my earliest songs. 4 Finger Pete and I returned to making music together and tracked "Effected by the Cure"—all about prescription pills and my experience with them. We called it "Effected" intentionally, to reference the drug Effexor. We recorded the song during my mental fog at that time. It was part of the journey to betterment—removing the Band-Aid and dealing with healing the open wounds.

This song spoke my truth. It even made the curriculum for a college course on prescription pills. Musically, it was made with purpose, and writing it helped me cope with the challenging withdrawal period.

Angela's dad, Al, was the father-in-law I always knew I'd have. He was a lieutenant colonel in the army who ran the *Stars and Stripes* paper and a radio station in Vietnam, where the radio DJ who inspired the movie *Good Morning, Vietnam* worked. Al is a first-generation Sicilian American raised in New Jersey who always tells it like it is—in that thick New Jersey accent.

We visited Al in Oahu, where he lives, and he told me in his strong, assertive voice, "Ben, you need to go back to school. I don't care what it is for, but you need to get a degree." When he said those words, I felt like shit. It was at a meal and in front of people. He was judging my actions. It was the right thing to say. I had stopped school to go to work when Kendo was born and never finished what I had started. He was looking out for me and, more importantly, for the future of his only daughter.

It was the first time someone had called me out about not finishing school. I disregarded it at the time with pride and a "fuck that"—but I didn't forget his advice. I heard his words in my head on the return flight. It wasn't going away because I hadn't finished what I started. I had a lot of catching up to do, and returning to college at twenty-eight was humbling.

I signed up for my first class back at college in my apartment on a dial-up connection. It was a music history class on classical music. I felt a surge of hope when I looked at my "schedule" for school. I had finished trimming the dead branches in my life. The next phase began—growth.

I started listening to Buddhist meditations led by Gil Fronsdal. I would sit in the stillness and enjoy the peace. I had always rejected meditation as something for pseudo-hippies, but once I gave it a chance, I realized how wrong I had been. It was training for the brain.

Meditation helped lead me down the path to come. I was drawn to it.

I worked real estate, was a full-time college student, and was in a band called Natural Fx at night. It was hectic, and I was proud of this. My weekends were spent with Kendo and Angela—living in Redwood Shores in a little apartment on the water. Although my schedule was filled with positive things, I was still way behind where I should have been—in my opinion.

At college, I walked around campus, aged almost thirty, and thought of my friends who had been with me ten years prior. I remembered the various places and classes we took together. In the same places now, all the faces looked much younger. I was the oldest student by far in nearly all my courses—almost a generation removed from most first-year students. No matter how awkward it felt, I had goals to achieve, but showing up every day was slightly embarrassing.

Anxiety still lurked in the shadows. Panic was still there underneath. I was sitting in the far corner of the classroom in a night class when the same feeling of panic I'd had so many years ago at St. Mary's hit me. There was a sense that I needed to get out of there. The powerful feeling of not belonging engulfed me as I looked around at kids in their late teens. I felt that horrible outsider feeling. I was facing the fear that had lain dormant. I just rode the wave of terror at my desk, frozen in place, looking down at an empty page in my notebook. Finally, the class was over—I didn't know if I could continue to face that level of fear.

I was scared. I went to a doctor and got some Xanax to continue with school. I took one daily for a few weeks, then half a pill for a few weeks. The meds helped since I didn't have the tools yet to do it on my own. Then I thought of an idea. In case of emergency, I would keep one pill in my wallet between a folded business card. I carried this pill everywhere. I rarely needed it, but like the paper bag for breathing as a kid, this security blanket helped me push on till I no longer needed it—but that would take some time. It had disintegrated many months before I was ready to throw it out.

I started running marathons with Dino's encouragement. He called me, saying he was running a full marathon in five weeks and suggesting I run a half-marathon. Until then, I hadn't run more than two miles since high school track, but it sounded like a challenge I was ready for. I went to the community track in Campbell, which was all-weather and had good buoyancy. I told myself I would enter the race if I could jog four miles without stopping. The laps ticked on very slowly as I got lost in Wyclef Jean's "Sweetest Girl" on my headphones on repeat. After my last lap around that track, I felt the rush of accomplishment as I slowed to a walk. I had proven to myself I was capable of much more than I thought. I signed up for my first half-marathon.

Over the next five weeks, I increased my weekly runs to ten miles. Then, with my feet on the start line in Palo Alto, California, I began my next phase in fitness. This race was my first organized event since high school track over ten years prior. I felt like I was going to die. I didn't think I would make the last mile, but I said to myself, "Fuck it. I'm still doing this if this is the last thing I do." I was willing to give my life for this. Something just wouldn't let me stop. I finished, my feet were bloody with busted blisters, and I could barely walk. I loved it.

I did four more half marathons—Rock 'n' Roll San Jose three times and the San Francisco half-marathon once. After that, I started training for a full marathon. I ran nineteen miles, from Campbell to Lexington Reservoir and back. When I stopped, I lost the drive to continue. I had done what I needed. I had nothing left to prove.

I applied the metaphor of running to my life. I kept picturing myself as a runner late to the race of life but slowly catching up and overtaking the pack. I was like that tree in the darkness, with barely any sunlight to its day. Then, gradually, it rose higher, gaining more traction every morning as it climbed above the forest's canopy, slowly catching up to the trees the same age. I was like the tree, finally getting enough sunlight.

Finding Purpose Through Pain

From your rock bottom moment, it won't be an overnight comeback. It will be slow, raw, and unglamorous. Make progress by showing up—one decision and one dead branch at a time.

You might find yourself cleaning up the wreckage and paying for your mistakes. You might be sitting in rooms with people you never thought you would be next to. These are the consequences of your past actions. Pay the debt and move on. You haven't failed if you are paying your debt, whether that is to society or even karmic. That is part of the cost and price you pay.

It will take time to remove all the crutches in place, whether that is substances or bad habits—just keep moving. I remember dumping the last of my prescription pills into the toilet and wondering if I was making a huge mistake. But an even bigger inner feeling was that of *If you don't do this, you will never reclaim your life*. Take the steps, make the change. Eventually, that past will turn to dust, dissolving away from your life, like those pills down the drain.

Be open to love and truth, maybe even from those who you would never expect to take guidance from. Have the courage to listen to your inner voice and follow its guidance. It is there; find it in the stillness.

I went back to junior college at nearly thirty, sitting frozen in panic among teenagers—but I kept showing up. One class at a time. You might be late to the race of life, but it's not over. Get on the track and catch up. Run your laps. Show up to class, work, and your passions. Refuse that which is killing you and accept that which positively challenges you.

THE INTERLUDE

THIS IS WHERE MY story changes.

From here forward, it's not just about survival.

It's about becoming, turning the fire into fuel.

It's about rising, not as the man I was, but as the man I was always meant to become.

It's about the nonstop pursuit of potential and the lessons I have learned along the way.

This is the start of what I have become.

CHAPTER 11

LIFE IS BEAUTIFUL

Life is beautiful, everything I do now has follow-through, because of you, everything around now is plentiful . . .

"*Life is Beautiful*"

I ARRIVED AT HENNESSY's house and there was a monk in an orange robe. I had never talked to a monk before, at least not past a quick hello. He was not a "typical" monk. He went by the name Dada Nabhaniilananda—aka "The Monk Dude"—and was as close to a rock star as a monk could be. He was from New Zealand and played the acoustic guitar confidently as we walked and sang kirtan music.

Kirtan is a spiritual music that is very calming. It helps prep the mind for meditation. You chant a mantra—in my case, "Baba Nam Keva Lam"—repetitively while walking in a circle at the same time. The activation of singing, walking, and clearing the mind is very powerful.

I felt like Dada had entered my life for a reason, so I stopped by the Jagriti (House of Worship and Meditation) where he lived to continue our conversation. A wave of calm washed over me when I entered the meditation room. I sensed spiritual energy. It was similar to the feeling in a beautiful cathedral. But there was an added element—meditation deepened the experience. After a few kirtan songs and guided meditation led by Dada, I left and drove home.

On my drive out of the Los Altos hills, I reflected on how calm my mind felt, and for the first time, I experienced a relaxing peace that I had previously only found in mind-altering substances. It was actually better—I had all my wits about me. There was also an element of counterculture; it was a place that was once again out of the mainstream.

A few weeks later, I returned and decided to commit to the meditation practice. Dada taught me the first meditative lesson, and with that, the next phase of my inner journey began. I started practicing meditation twice a day—about forty-five minutes in the morning and forty-five minutes at night.

I was cleaning the window to my soul. I was going inward in the same way I do when making music. I was entering the inner depths of the mind and finding growth, healing, and insight. I started performing with Dada all over the Bay Area. He would sing and play guitar, and I would play the djembe—an African hand drum. We recorded albums, audiobooks, and guided meditations together. I meditated twice a day, no matter what, and continued to feel in control of my path. Dada and I recorded a sunrise and sunset meditation—and I listened to them daily for years. They are on YouTube and are a great way to relax, if you are interested.

I started feeling like my therapy sessions no longer gave me the insight they once did. I would go only once a month, but even at that frequency, it felt like little was left to discuss. The days of excitement to drive to the session and share were in the past. Finally, Dr. Elmare said, "I think our work is done." It was time. I was now ready to go free and thrive in life.

I was able to love my day and, most importantly, myself. I started having positive dreams, feeling excited to fall asleep. Previously, my dreams had been filled with night terrors.

Angela and I moved into the same house on Saratoga Avenue in West San Jose where I had lived before, but everything kept improving this time. The place of former trauma and darkness was now a palace of growth and love. The garage was a music studio and meditation room. The backyard became a garden and a meditative walking path.

Natural Fx—the band I was in—did a Halloween show at the Brookdale Lodge opening for Del the Funky Homosapien and Living Legends. It was epic—a packed house and great vibes. I recalled how, fifteen years earlier, I had thought of Del as the epitome of cool while flipping through skate magazines—and now I was sharing the stage with him. I walked into the venue for a soundcheck, and the sound guy for the concert thought I was the headliner who had so greatly influenced my teenage self. After Del did that song with Gorillaz, "Clint Eastwood," he became internationally known. My favorite moment with Natural Fx was that moment on the stage at the Brookdale Lodge.

Natural Fx was climbing through the Bay Area music scene. We were regularly opening for more significant acts when they came to town. My bandmates and I, like most bands, had run into creative differences. It was time to move on. I remember feeling lost and having emotions like a relationship breakup for a few days. My identity was becoming ingrained in the constant practice and endless shows. Natural Fx had run its course.

I was ready to complete my first solo project. I made a few songs, called a promoter I had met from the Natural Fx shows, and booked my first solo performance. It was nerve-racking, thinking I would be alone on stage. Also, I had only a few songs that were mine and barely knew the words. I had a catalog of five songs and needed to play all of them. I finally stepped onto the stage alone. I could hide no longer. It was my time, and I had a direction. I was entering a new phase of life—in multiple ways.

After almost a decade of trying to convince Angela to marry me, she randomly called from work and said she had found the perfect little white chapel at Cavallo Point in Sausalito. We were about to be done "playing house"—as I call the trial phase of partnership—and ready for the real thing at the age of thirty-one.

I wrote a song for Angela called "Life is Beautiful." I had a cellist, a viola player, and an opera singer record it—all of whom I met through Dada. Dino and 4 Finger Pete also contributed to the music. I surprised Angela, who didn't know I was working on the song, and played it for our first dance at our wedding. I was hitting a fantastic stride, and life was becoming something different. Life was beautiful.

The housing market had taken a massive dive in 2008, and by 2012, it was in the final moments of the downturn. I told Angela it was now or never. We bought our home at the bottom of the market—before escrow closed, it was worth much more. The house was in Willow Glen, bank-owned, and the previous owner had messed it up—intentionally. When I walked in, I knew it was perfect. It was missing everything. There was missing carpet, holes in the floor, termites, and holes in the walls. The kitchen was gutted, the roof leaked everywhere, windows were broken, and a squatter lived next door. Trauma was present. You could feel it. When I walked into the living room, I saw the door to the somewhat ominous basement. I went downstairs to the basement, and the room smelled funny. There was also graffiti on the walls. It had one small boarded-up window at the top of the wall aligned with the asphalt driveway outside. I knew this would be my studio, my space to create like never before. I had to accept that this would cement my life as a solo artist—there would be no band practice here—it was too small for a band. Also, the only access was through my family's home, so musicians couldn't come and go like they had ever since I started making music. Now, concrete walls surrounded me—no distractions. I had yet to release any solo music online. One man's music would reach the world from the isolated beginnings of those four underground concrete walls. Over the next decade, this would be where I would create, mix, and release over 100 songs.

I was still acclimating to my life in progress. I would have brief insecure moments that had me questioning myself. I now had a lot of weight on my shoulders. I was a realtor, musician, student, homeowner, husband, and father. It was a lot, and life was not without reminders of the past trauma. I was still very much aware of my anxiety, which would occasionally show itself, humbling me. For example, when Angela was seven months pregnant, we took a trip to the big island of Hawaii. We wanted to take Kendo, just the three of us, for a final trip before our daughter was born. On the plane, I felt anxiety kick in. I started to feel like I wasn't good enough for all this and that I didn't belong.

The feeling of being trapped in the plane crept over me, and I started having another panic attack. The thought of not being in control and in this plane brought fear into my mind. All I could do was close my eyes and hope it would pass without me dying. I felt this life I had created was too good. The happiness was too right. It had happened so many times before: when life got too good, that evil force took it away. This time, though, nothing happened. There was no darkness after. It was just a residual effect of past trauma. The old wounds would reveal themselves in a last-gasp attempt to engulf me in the flames.

During the whole trip to Hawaii, I kept this inside—I even looked up boats to take back to California to avoid facing getting on the plane again. Sitting in my hotel, I finally decided to meditate for the whole ride back on the plane. I would go internal and face the fear. I would do what I had done so many times since the moment of change at twenty-eight. I would fight against the evil unknown. I would finally capture the eternal fire that burned inside. Fire can burn us, or it can fuel us. It can destroy but also help grow. Fire can clear out the brush and allow the large trees to thrive. The redwoods can handle the fire, and now so could I.

I had my last panic attack on that plane over ten years before writing this book. I respect anxiety enough to know that it can always come back. Anxiety and the power of the ocean come to mind as both deserving respect. They could have their way with you at any time. But we can confidently move forward knowing we understand them better and learn from them. Through complex life experiences, we can learn about ourselves and better prepare for difficult moments ahead. With that knowledge alone, I find comfort.

My daughter Gianna was born shortly after we moved into our home in Willow Glen. Having a daughter, I saw every day was different in so many ways. I no longer needed to condense all my guidance into a few hours. I also didn't have the intense feelings of loss I felt when I needed to drop Kendo off. Further, I was now a man. I had turned my life around and had already been a father for over a decade. I was living stably, and it showed. I selected Moses to be my daughter's godfather because he had always been a stable peer while I was going through chaos. He was always there for me, even when I couldn't be for him.

Full-time parenting is more challenging in different ways—there are fewer breaks. I was hitting an ever-increasing stride in music, so Gianna would ride with me everywhere while I worked on the latest song. She was raised in my music studio and was the only person to hear my musical progress daily.

Gianna and I would listen to my new music in the car, evaluate the progress, and analyze when a song was done. I taught her how to find the authenticity in a vocal and recognize when a singer doesn't quite have it. She was living deep into the details of music and understanding the elements that make successful musicians.

I have an essential message for young fathers: give your children time and attention. The effort spent during the child-rearing years will reap significant rewards. I have no regrets for all my sacrifices in this one aspect of life. Those who see their children in condensed time frames must cherish every minute. There is value in the specialness of not being with them constantly. Your kids will remember the effort and time you gave to them. They will gain strength from your love and support when you are not with them. It isn't easy. It is challenging to deal with exes. Difficult to drive long distances. Difficult to deal with the new spouse. It is challenging to divide up holidays. But more than anything, it's worth it.

You won't regret what you did. You will regret what you didn't do. Take the time to develop a relationship with your kids. Mothers, please understand that your kids need to feel the love and support of their father when possible. I know it's hard, but it is our responsibility as parents to give this gift to our kids whenever possible. We don't want our children to need to take sides or feel the burden of hate toward the other parent. That is not fair. It was you who had the relationship first. Now, let them have their own relationship with that parent. They can make their judgments in time.

Full-time parenting, I found, had a different challenge. The time blends together, and memorable moments are less prioritized. Too quickly, life can become routine, and we can get caught up in being "too busy." All too soon, the kids will be out of the house, and the time they live with you will be only memories when they go to college.

I graduated *summa cum laude* from college, with scholarships, with a degree in psychology. As a kid, I never did too well in school. I never had a moment of recognition. This was just what I needed. I was passionate about school and cared. When I was younger, I had no idea that the only thing I was missing was taking pride in my work. I learned that if I do something, I do it A+. Now, that was and is my mantra. I also received academic scholarship money—I was getting paid to attend school. It was ten years after my peers, but I handled business at an A+ level. I was growing more every day—achieving the goals I had set for myself.

Finding Purpose Through Pain

Finding your own version of inner peace is vital. Meditation does that. Therapy can do that. Deep prayer can do that. It can be whatever version works for you. It has little to do with religion and can transfer to whatever ideology you connect to. The important part is connecting to the stillness and the clarity within it.

You carry a lot of roles, labels, and responsibilities. The foundation of duties is in the internal mind. Whatever label or role you play, you will function better with meditation. The same could be said for therapy, or deep, focused prayer. These are categories some turn away from in some default, not-for-me response, without ever giving it a chance. The reality is that when you open yourself up to progress, then all other categories of life can thrive. I experienced my last panic attack on that flight to Hawaii. On the flight home—committed to overcoming the panic—I meditated the entire time. This moment marked the end of a decades-long struggle. That's the power of internal practice. Stillness reveals what the noise tried to bury. When you stop running from the inner work, your outer world starts to shift as well.

The spiritual and internal work benefits you, your career, your family, and your relationships. I returned to the same house that ended my full-time life with my son and turned it into a meditation room, complete with a garden path and music studio. I was committed to the multifaceted path of progress. Build your inner peace like you would your body—through consistency, and focus.

CHAPTER 12

I RISE

Relax, it's calm, peace, storm. Wait for the war, wrecked from the shore. Heavy rain when it pour, inner mind war. Bust through the door, never rest till I'm sore.

"I Rise"

I RELEASED MY FIRST solo album as Ben Barbic. It was titled *Improve the Silence*. I started recording it in our West San Jose rental and finished it in the basement of our new home in Willow Glen. I had 4 Finger Pete help add instrumentation and provide mixing guidance—remotely.

We sent the session back and forth to work in our own spaces. The responsibility was mine to bring projects to a conclusion. My music had become highly personal, and I was comfortable enough to embrace it.

Some people pointed to the sacrifice I made when my son was born, citing that as the moment my dreams died—they were wrong. My responsibility fueled my progress. I just needed to push more. The road I'm about to describe keeps me fulfilled and making music. My music has limitless potential. Every day of every year, I climb higher. Everything I have done in music results from the opportunities technology has given me. I was able to connect with the entire world, all starting in my basement studio. If I dared to put myself out there, my dreams could burn brighter. If I could deal with sleepless nights and creatively limited days, I could reach whatever heights my music could take me. I could build my music online and distribute it to the entire world.

Online would get me where I needed to be. I started with ten followers and used an app with an autoresponder when someone followed me. Additionally, I followed people I thought would appreciate my music—some of them followed back. Then, I would send them one of my songs. I followed 100 people every morning. Perhaps ten would follow back, and then a few of those would comment that they liked my music. After a few months, it started catching on, and I got positive responses. My confidence grew over time with very little criticism and many notes of support.

I worked in my damp, concrete-walled underground basement at night, after Gianna and Angela went to bed. I created music every night from 9:00 p.m. to about 2:00 a.m. Regardless of whether I had to be up at 6:00 a.m., this was my routine. I focused on improving as an artist and connecting with listeners, producers, artists, and DJs.

I got my first significant radio connection through social media. Rick Levine, host of *Inside the ICEBOX* on 102.7 FM in Canada, found me on social media and believed in my music. He played my song while saying, "There are some really great musicians on Twitter, and this is one of them. Here is Ben Barbic with 'Radio.'"

> *I like to take it slow, and I flow through the cool breeze, feel the wind pass, and I kicking up the brown leaves.*
>
> *"Radio"*

After this, I kept at the online promotion. I got a few interview requests. I was incredibly nervous on the first one, speaking fast for the first few minutes. I thought, *They must have made a mistake booking me. I have nothing to say*. It filled my mind. But once that passed, it got easier. I played music and interviewed on South African, English, and Indonesian radio stations. Up until this point, all my musical progress was with technology. It was me recording, mixing, and mastering in my basement, then promoting myself with the tools I found independently on my computer—tools we all have. I just kept going, every day.

Opportunity knocked when I least expected it. My teenage friend Frankie had moved to New York City years earlier to pursue a career in entertainment, and I had only heard from him off and on since he moved. He let me know that he could get a song picked up for a TV show called *Knockout*. I wrote a song called "Fighter" and sent it to Frankie, who shared it with a music executive.

This was my first time having someone in the music business listen to my music and appreciate it. When I spoke with the executive on the phone, I felt nervous. I hadn't encountered a potential entry into the world of musical greatness until this moment. He represented my first taste of full-time involvement in the music business.

The executive and I started working on making the most of the tune. I kept redoing the lyrics, per his request. Eventually, the song reached a point where he was satisfied, and we planned a trip to New York to record it and launch my career. I feverishly worked on pushing my craft while I waited for the day to leave. I practiced my flow endlessly whenever I had free time. I was training like a fighter and ready to nail it when I arrived in New York.

Two days before I was supposed to leave, I saw a missed call from the producer and anxiously checked my voicemail for the instructions for the upcoming trip. It was far from what I thought. "Ben, we've decided not to go forward with the project. Wish you the best." That was it. The trip was canceled—no further explanation was given, and no follow-up call was made. My dream recording session was off the table. I didn't hear from anyone on that side for quite some time. I got a little taste of the higher level of music, and as quickly as the door opened, it slammed shut. This became a consistent theme I faced in the music industry. Thoughts ran through my head about what to do. I felt a massive letdown as I sat on my front steps, knowing my dream of musical glory had been dashed.

I had been feeling off, and with this letdown to my musical progress, I took notice. My body was screaming from all angles—bulging discs in my back and neck, and constant heart palpitations. After getting some bloodwork done, I was informed I had Hashimoto's thyroiditis, an autoimmune disease. I sat while my doctor showed me the holes in my thyroid—my immune system was confused and attacking my thyroid. At first, I was a bit scared, then I asked a simple question, "Do I need to take medication?"

She said, "Not if you can keep it under control." That was all I needed. I could do what I do with this thing as well.

Getting that diagnosis didn't just name the illness—it named the enemy I'd been fighting in silence. Suddenly, all the times I felt overly tired made sense. I realized why I often experienced heart palpitations, a low pulse, and overall fatigue. I now knew who my enemy was, and I was determined to attack it back. I didn't sit in sadness; I sat thinking two things. First, *I'm not taking pills unless I must*. Second, *I will research the shit out of this and make the changes myself.*

I needed to take out gluten, soy, and other foods that could keep me from having these symptoms and slow the deterioration of my thyroid. I was determined not to take the thyroid medicine. I started running daily, at least two miles, and slowly regained my energy. I didn't let my health control me; I flipped that shit and made the moves full throttle to fix the thing. I was becoming a fighter against that which attacked me. I was not the victim—now I was in control.

I took the same approach with music; I was going to do it with or without opportunities. I drew strength from the rejection of the failed attempt to go to New York and drafted a tune called "I Rise." I called 4 Finger Pete and, with his help, put out my first single since the *Improve the Silence* album. This tune was different—it had more life and fire vocally. I had fuel behind it and a sense of urgency to create it. It represented climbing out of physical, mental, and musical frustration. I kept picturing myself busting through the door of the music industry. Nothing was going to stop my progress forward.

"I Rise" had a different tone and passion to the lyrics—the audience connected to it. I was getting closer to my authentic self. My music started to connect more. I wasn't fully there, but I was closer to harnessing my inner fire. I was closer to embracing the wounds of the past and being honest.

Finding Purpose Through Pain

You don't need permission to begin. Just start unapologetically. You don't need a record deal, a producer, an engineer, or even a tour. Just start with whatever tools you have in whatever you are passionate about doing. Don't ever succumb to the excuse of waiting for anything. I've heard people rhyme using just a five-gallon paint bucket to make the beat and rapping their lyrics. That would be the definition of having nothing. You have more than that, and someone is out there right now on the streets of many cities with a bucket and a voice, playing their heart out.

You might be building in the stillness of the night when you should be asleep. I created my first solo album in a damp basement studio while my family slept. I was tired but relentless. I gained fuel by knowing I worked while most slept. If you're tired and scattered, good—it proves you're hungry and willing to sacrifice. You might get close to the dream only to watch the door slam shut. This is also good; it increases the drive to get to where you're going, more fuel. I got a call canceling a dream opportunity with a prominent music executive two days before I was to leave. From that pain, I created "I Rise." It was a song of authenticity where I found purpose in the pain of rejection.

It's only too late when you're dead. If you're breathing, you have time. Rejection is vital to get over quickly. It helps you and is needed for progress. When you get rejected, take the loss and keep going.

There are other battles of the inner mind war that are invisible to everyone but you. The dream might be carried for years or even decades without outside recognition. That's the way it works. Do it for you and keep going. Don't get fooled into thinking one day you will be discovered. That is a lottery win. For most, including you, just keep going. Doesn't matter if you are at the top of the charts or have one listener who shares your last name. Keep going. It's for more than those accolades. This is for your soul and finding your purpose.

CHAPTER 13

UNKNOWN ROAD

Man, I take my own road, embrace the unknown.
Spend life in my phone trying to maintain my home.
"Unknown Road"

I HAD FOCUS NOW. I could go into the studio and capture the essence of a song and deliver the lyrics. I never really stick to written lyrics. Having it all written out puts too much confinement on the art. I like to write out one verse, max. I only use the opening line or two to get things rolling. Then, with a rhyming dictionary open on the far side of the screen, I feel my way to the lyrics. I like to shape songs like that. It keeps my words authentic and believable. I can perfectly blend line upon line through repetition, writing as I go until all the lyrics have meaning.

Sometimes it takes me weeks to find the correct lyrics and cadence. Occasionally, it all flows out in one sitting. It's not true that an artist's work is never done. It's a wrap when the lyrics feel right and there are no weak lines. I might have to rewrite the verse and chorus five times, maybe more. But I know when it is done. I think that is a very critical part of writing and composing music.

On "Unknown Road," the words just flowed out. The song was completed in one day, with only a minor clean-up needed to fix misspoken lines and things. I always love it when that happens, when I know what I'm supposed to say and how.

I flipped on the Rode NTK mic, opened a page of a few lyrical sentences I had written, and felt driven to create.

It was genuine and honest. It was my life then and still is—"taking the unknown road" even became my mantra. Occasionally, a song will come out of my soul unexpectedly. This was one of them, representing a significant turning point in my flow style, cadence, and identity within the music. Finally, I was able to capture authenticity in my words. Pure me was pouring out. As the next few years progressed, I started to get better and better at finding that authenticity. As with "Good Times" from a decade and a half before, if you listen to "Unknown Road," you can hear my arrival. Genuine, honest, and like a greyhound being let out of the starting gate.

This was the first time I removed the safety net of other people. It was my moment of musical courage. It took a decade and a half for me to get there. I was now ready. Confidently, I charged forward. It was as if the stored energy of my music was finally released. The floodgates of truth had opened. I found my genuine self in the music, and it shined through. I had returned to the source that compelled me to write that original "Good Times" tune.

I sent the song to Frankie, and it wasn't long before I got a call that changed my life. He said, "I showed 'Unknown Road' to Phil, bro. We're gonna set you up for some meetings with the record labels and some producers. You need to get the fuck out here now! I'm gonna buy your ticket for Monday. You good?" I only had one answer to give.

Two days later, I boarded a flight to NYC. I had only flown by myself one other time, and that was a flight from San Jose to Hawaii to meet Angela years earlier. There was no time to worry about a fear of flying, though. Somehow, the situation waiting for me when I got to NYC erased that fear. It became evident that as my self-confidence rose, my anxiety fell—something I am now very aware of. My self-confidence is so tied to anxiety. I wasn't in the wrong place. I was entering my world—the place I belonged.

Even though I was alone on a plane with strangers, I didn't feel alone internally. I was becoming more aligned with my genuine self. The inner darkness wasn't there.

As the plane was descending into New York, I was having visions of just how far I'd come, and the rarity of what was ahead. I played Andrea Bocelli's "Con te partirò" the whole way down during the landing. The song's drama helped me cope with the significance of the situation. I was a bit emotional. I felt like I was riding on the wings of my family. They were all there with me. Those alive and those I had lost, I felt them all with me. I felt guided by their love and support. This became a common theme in my life.

On the bus ride from JFK Airport to Manhattan, I saw my future get closer as I approached the immensity of the city at night. I thought about how I was there to fulfill a dream. Like so many others before me on the NYC journey, the talent I had cultivated for as long as I could remember got me to that place on that day. I shared the thought of generations of artists arriving in this magical city from humble beginnings. I went from the basement to the Big Apple.

I met Frankie in the middle of Times Square and felt a sense of how far we had come. Two friends, almost twenty years after high school, in one of the most visited and admired places on earth. We talked about the various meetings I would have over the coming days as we walked casually past all the iconic Manhattan spots. Settling into his apartment, around the corner from Bad Boys studios, I was excited for what awaited me in the coming days. I knew my life would change.

I had an in-person meeting with musical accountant legend Bert Padell the following day. Bert had helped develop the careers of many musical legends and was willing to meet and talk with me. Just saying "I'm here for a meeting with Bert Padell" to the receptionist was empowering. I sat with Bert in his conference room, which he used as an office. He talked to me about his background and asked about mine. He also asked me why I wanted a music career and asked, "How old are you?" When I said thirty-five, he replied, "Too bad you didn't come to me when you were twenty-nine! Hahaha." I had passed the glorious window of youth. The truth was that I hadn't been ready at twenty-nine. He said it somewhat in jest, but there was also a reality to it. He asked me to come back with my demo reel, and he would give it to his friends for a listen. That friend list was a "who's who" of prominent label owners. I left with a new level of swagger. I became closer to my ideal self after that meeting. Sometimes, just showing up is enough of a win to propel you forward. I was talking to Bert Padell! The guy in a Biggie Smalls lyric.

The chaos of NYC and the high-level meetings I was scheduling relaxed me. I feel most comfortable when things are hectic. I think it goes back to my youth and the chaos of life—that, and frequently going very fast on a motorcycle. While I was a kid, my dad would take me to school on the back of his bike. We would split lanes down Highway 17 in the Santa Cruz Mountains and go fast. I remember road trips on the bike when I would lift my head to see over his shoulder—often, the speedometer would read over 100 miles per hour. I would start singing to myself and feel incredibly relaxed. This feeling began in my earliest days when things were intense. I relax. I often channel the same feeling when I perform on stage, lift weights, mountain bike, wakeboard, or engage in any extreme activity, and a lot is on the line. When it's game time or a severe situation is unfolding—such as an accident or natural disaster—my world becomes clear, focused, and calm. This trip to New York was a wonderful reminder of who I am and how I thrive in chaotic and intense situations.

Next, I walked across town to meet Devo Springsteen. Devo won a Grammy for producing the best rap song of 2006, "Diamonds from Sierra Leone." I must admit I was nervous about this meeting. He was the biggest producer I had ever met. When we sat down at a Pret-a-Manger, I had doubts—thinking I was too old for this. Unlike with Bert, my age was no factor for Devo. He told me straight up I could have a career in music with my talent. He said he wanted to work on "Move On" and "Where the Dreams

Sail"—a very emotional tune I had written a few months earlier.

> *I'm cut from a different cloth. Sitting still means getting soft. Train stops, getting off. And where my homies now? They not around. It seems I'm literally and physically I'm underground. Dreams about to drown. But I'm just getting hotter. Why do I even bother if I never gonna prosper?*
>
> *"Where the Dreams Sail"*

I met Phil Caruso at a steakhouse in Manhattan around 10:00 p.m. You can get to know Phil by watching the TV show *So I Married a Mobster*. We had the "usual table" in the restaurant's corner and were treated like kings. The waiter treated us like "the Don" himself was there. We casually discussed over dinner if I wanted to get signed to a major or an independent record label. I said, "A major label," and he said, "OK, we will put you in touch with a few different guys." Unreal! After dinner, he said, "Alright, Ben, you go this way, we go that. I'll talk to you soon." I walked back to Frankie's apartment, full of hope. The city of dreams was embracing me. I was gaining such confidence, growing stronger.

I boarded my flight home the next day, ready for more. I didn't even pay attention to the fact that I was on a plane.

I felt the same on the bus as I did on the plane—no more concern for travel. No more anxiety. The success was my remedy for panic. I took the energy that NYC possesses with me. My dreams had started to become a reality.

When I returned home, everything seemed more manageable. The intensity made things simple. My real estate career started to take off. I was excited to meet people. I gained so much confidence through the music that it translated to all aspects of my life. I wasn't writing heavy lyrics during my downtime at open houses anymore. I created fun environments with music during the open houses I was hosting. I was excited for people to walk through the door. People started wanting to work with me. I always had my secret life of music, but there was no way to hide it anymore. If you googled me, more music than real estate came up. This was freeing. I was proud of it. I could embrace the duality of my existence.

I live in two worlds simultaneously. During the day, I am a father, husband, and realtor. At night, I enter my basement and become an artist. It begins by opening my sticker-covered door and walking downstairs. Album covers, past show flyers, and mementos on my journey help me flip my mind into the creative space. I channel that inner creativity and stay in my basement. No phone calls are taken, and my mind drifts into the place of safety and familiarity that music brings me. I decided to call my basement studio Where Dreams Sail Studios. The place where dreams are alive—where musical creation constantly introduces me to life on the unknown road.

The opportunities of the NYC trip fell apart one by one. Bert was unable to get a taker on my music. The major labels liked my music but weren't ready to sign me. A few weeks later, I read of Phil's arrest in the *New York Post*. He had been under surveillance for weeks and went away for years, so that also bore no fruit. I still had plans for working with Devo, but even those started to drag on.

These were opportunities presented that didn't pan out. In life, I had grown accustomed to rejection. Real estate is a tricky business. Family and friends can use other realtors. It hurts. It's a personal rejection, no doubt about it. I had gotten used to pivoting off of setbacks—learning from the pain. Life and work had shown me to make purpose out of the losses. Why didn't I get the listing? Why didn't they sign me on the label? The answers to these questions help personal growth.

I gained confidence from this original trip. Even though nothing panned out, it helped my journey. Flip it. Rejection is a time for growth. When things don't work out, find the meaning in the result. Don't blame others. Go internal. What could I have done better? It was time to continue my progress and push forward.

Finding Purpose Through Pain

The moment you find your authenticity—your truth—doors start to open. When this happens, it is not random. It's proof that you are stepping into alignment. And when those doors open, walk through them. It could take a very long time for opportunity to appear, but it will if you stick with it. Stay ready. Keep pursuing progress, crave it. One moment of truth can shift everything, like it did for me with "Unknown Road."

When you level up, it won't feel comfortable. It might even be overwhelming. The good news is that life gets better on the other side of that moment of unsettling energy. What was once intimidating begins to feel normal and like you belong. You will feel more comfortable as you become exposed to higher levels of talent, skill, and even financial abundance. Confidence will replace hesitation. As you rise, your fear shrinks. You are too focused on your purpose to let fear into your mind.

There will be a shift when you courageously take the step. You don't need to be certain; just trust in the process and progress within the opportunity. Picture that next level waiting for your arrival. Keep climbing.

CHAPTER 14

WHERE SHOULD I GO?

And I can hear the beat, the running of my heart. I'm hearing that it's calling for me, wishing that I start. And I can feel the riddim, or I can sing the blues. I know that in life sometimes we all have to choose. And I can feel the stage moving on again. I'm ready to begin, spit it, run with my friends. And I can hear the voice of my inner demons go, I know exactly where it is that I should go.

"Where Should I Go"

I'M CONSTANTLY EVALUATING WHERE I am and where I want to get to. I'm always trying to grow. It's easy to stay in the shadows. A tree can blend into the shade of other trees and never be noticed. It seems safe and doesn't take effort. But if a redwood seedling doesn't stretch for all the sunlight it can, it will eventually lose the last of its light. The nearby trees will take it all. It will be a shadow in plain view. Invisible in the crowd. If redwoods don't grow, they also won't survive the fire. They won't have the strength to withstand what life dishes out. They won't have the power to battle the flames and will eventually die.

Dreams can die, too. If we don't grow, life can pass us by, lost in shade and decay. If we don't step out of the shadows and embrace the light, we are on a path to a slow death. If we don't dare to pursue our dreams, then a part of us is lost for the remainder of our journey in life. It is scary to put ourselves out there, to be the tree that stands out. If we are noticed, people can criticize us. They can gossip and demean everything we stand for. It is scary. But not as much as one would think. I see many artists who never put anything out, giving me countless reasons why they are happy to keep it all to themselves. On evaluation, I've yet to see that logic ring true. It's a coping mechanism. Sharing with the world is essential if you love something and spend endless hours pursuing it. The world is filled with like-minded people, regardless of personal taste.

There is an audience for your craft—a community that will embrace you. Don't be too scared to be you.

A local cinematographer named Alan and I crafted a music video dealing with our calling in life. As I wrote, I pictured a life of regret, not doing what I wanted with my time on this planet. Regret was my greatest fear, that sense of life passing me by while I wasted my days. We laid out the screenplay in my backyard, and then I crafted the song "Too Scared," having 4 Finger Pete add in the guitar and piano.

> *I can't sleep at night, fight never gone, never give up, always move on, always keep on, I. . ., take my head off the pillow and I, flip back on the light, look to my left, then I rise. I'm like a fighter every night fight. I won't hide, bout to take flight, every night type. Then go inside, chaotic mind, failed, retried, ditch the excuse, don't make me choose, I will not lose, push through, used, grew.*
>
> *"Too Scared"*

"Get your passport ready. We are headed to Mexico City in two days," Frankie said in his inimitable style, almost finding joy in my lack of international experience. Frankie had asked Alan and me to be part of a production team for an event in Mexico City. I would be an artist representative and conduct the English interviews.

Buckling my seat belt on the plane, I reflected on how far removed I now was from panic attacks. Life was not passing me by. I was now traveling worldwide, solo, under extreme pressure, and succeeding.

With our VIP badges in hand, we worked the event in the heart of Mexico City at Zócalo (Plaza de la Constitución), frantically interviewing participants and speakers among the thousands of people. Unfortunately, we had a lot of technical issues with our audio and video, as we were using a new setup, and some pieces were malfunctioning, but we made it work in the end.

On the final night, sitting in the dimly lit Hotel Geneve Telephone Bar, Alan said, "You were so cool under pressure when the equipment went bad. I want you to be a part of our movie sound team." I had no desire to do sound for a movie, but I knew what would happen if I did it. He said they would put me in the film and feature my music. Again, it was about taking every opportunity I could, and they seemed to present themselves at a breakneck pace.

While preparing to leave for the movie shoot, I finished a song called "Where Should I Go" with a producer out of French Guiana named Israel Rinaldo, who produced reggae and hip-hop music. He was living in Australia and reached out on SoundCloud. He said he liked my style and wanted to work on some music. The first song we made was "Fight Through the Storm," which did quite well.

It even got me a radio interview in South Africa on an African Crest Radio station. With the success of the first song, we then did "Where Should I Go," which was more of a reggae/ hip-hop collaboration. It was a complicated tune lyrically—my fastest rhyming up to that point—and the riddim connected well with my vocal style. The song was about knowing where I'm trying to get to, going for it, and learning the moves I should make next.

"Riddim" is a term for the music bed, or instrumental, in reggae music. In reggae and dancehall, you often take the "riddim" and have multiple singers' voices on the same music, calling it a "riddim album." The singers all make their own version of the song, and it's a great way to hear how different singers interpret the same music.

The movie shoot was scheduled for three weeks in Miami. I was amped. The day before we were going to leave, Alan called the whole team to a last-minute meeting. He said the financier had backed out, and the movie shoot was canceled. Additionally, he mentioned that if he could convince the star, Julio Bracho, to come to San Jose, we could still film the movie—if we were in. I had planned my life around the few-week shoot, so I was in. Julio was also in, so the movie began.

We traveled around San Jose with telenovela (TV drama) stars Julio Bracho and Jullye Giliberti. I held the mic boom for all the scenes. If you don't know what

I'm talking about, it's the guy with the long pole and the furry things on the end. Not only that, but I was also the sound guy who didn't speak Spanish. So here is Ben, a realtor by day, musician by night, and now a sound man of a Spanish-language film—who can't say he's ever done movie sound before—dangling a mic inches above famous actors. I wondered how strange it would be for one of my real estate clients to see me in this alternative world.

Julio thought it was funny to have a sound guy who didn't speak Spanish for a movie in Spanish. One scene was in a church in San Jose called Sacred Heart of Jesus. I was standing in a pew in complete silence as Julio delivered his most intense lines of the movie so far. My arms were about to fall off as he quietly spoke his lines. Part of the learning curve of movie sound is realizing when you picked the wrong arm position to hold the boom mic. Your arms start giving out while holding a mic right above the lead actor's face. I was sweating profusely while I held my arms in place, constantly thinking how close I was to dropping that thing right on his head as he delivered a stunning performance. I was mesmerized by the quality of his acting in such close proximity. The stillness of the church just amplified my up-close experience of acting at its finest. It was Julio and me—inches away—barely out of the camera shot. I learned at that moment how amazing it can be to watch good acting live.

After he nailed it, we went to a restaurant down the street, and the whole neighborhood stared at him. It was a predominantly Mexican neighborhood, and everyone recognized him. It was my first time walking with someone everyone knew and was staring at. It was fun. It felt like even eating tacos turned into a spectacle. I told Julio his scene was impressive, and he replied, "How do you know? You don't speak Spanish." I told him it was all in the expressions and energy. I think he liked that, and we became friendly after that.

In the next scene, Julio walked into a music studio and said to the lead actress, Jullye Giliberti, "This is our new amazing talent," pointing into the vocal booth and talking about me. While in the vocal booth, I delivered the first verse to "Where Should I Go."

After I performed the song for the take, Julio and Jullye stood there, and Julio said, "Why the hell are you here doing this little movie with us?"

Finding Purpose Through Pain

There is a slow death to feeling safe, hidden, and unheard. You must fight against that fate. The longer you sit in the shadows, the dimmer your fire becomes. You weren't built to blend in. You were built to grow boldly, visibly, and with purpose. I had never done movie sound or even held a boom, and I didn't speak Spanish—yet there

I was holding a mic over Julio Bracho's head and hoping my arms wouldn't collapse. I didn't fit in, but I didn't need to. Ask yourself: Are you stepping into what scares you, or is life passing you by because you avoid the pressure?

Growth doesn't come from perfect conditions. It comes from pressure, rejection, practice, failure, and more. When things get intense and uncomfortable, when life tests your sense of self, step into it. If it's art, put it out and keep moving on to the next. Whether it's music, writing, business, performing, or pursuing your calling, lean into the chaos. That is where you will transform and sharpen the quickest. You don't need to be ready, just be willing.

CHAPTER 15

NOT A GAME

I knowing it's not the same, pushing it forward more than trained, giving it all I got, it's not a game.
"Not a Game"

After the movie finished shooting, I booked Suspect Studios in San Jose for a session—the same studio where we had shot the film. I had a verse in a draft song called "Not a Game" that was about as fast as things could get. This was the accumulation of fast rhyming that had all started from that initial Young MC "Fastest Rhyme" tune I memorized as a youth. I had been working on fast rhyming since that initial introduction to it. Now, I had my own fastest rhyme—I wanted to return to the origins of this session. The days of listening to the quick verses of Young MC and Treach in my youth left a lasting impression. Decades later, I still love how intense, fast rhyming flips things so quickly. You must listen many times to understand it, like deciphering a lyrical puzzle, and constantly rewind the song to gain a deeper understanding.

I entered the vocal booth excited and prepared, having practiced and rehearsed the verse for a week before the session. When the engineer pressed RECORD, I flipped the switch and felt that feeling of gametime. I delivered half of it exactly how I wanted, but asked him to punch me in for the second half.

"Punching in," when recording vocals, is to sing over an already laid vocal. Then the engineer starts recording the new vocal at the exact mark musicians have set—usually between sentences or another marker, so it isn't noticeable to the audience.

When I told the house audio engineer to punch me in, he said in a somewhat condescending tone, "There's no way you gonna hit that." My counter was, "I record every day, trust me, punch me in."

I got the second part on one try—it was a wrap.

Moving forward, I began collaborating with people all over the world. I made a song with an Italian singer,

Maggiore, from Brindisi. We connected online and, through Google Translate, were able to communicate and create a song—"Paradiso Intorno." Next, I heard a song on Pandora I loved called "Life I Lead." I reached out to the singer Konu, who was willing to work together. Konu, from Hawaii, and I recorded "Trenches of Shadows," produced again by Israel Rinaldo. Israel lived in Paris by this point and asked me to come out for a month and record. It was intimidating and difficult to justify to my family, but I kept considering the opportunity.

I got a call from Frankie saying I was cleared to go to a private event for the president of Ghana at the time, John Dramani Mahama. They were trying to fill the party with noteworthy people in entertainment, and I somehow got the green light although I was far from famous. I headed down to Beverly Hills for the event at a prominent movie director's mansion in the hills. On arrival, I looked at the guest list, and the name below where mine should have been was Calvin Broadus (Snoop Dogg). My name wasn't there for some reason, but the director's wife came up and said, "There you guys are!" and took us in to the party. As we mingled poolside, the director's wife came up to Frankie and me and said, "How does this work?" Frankie said, "What do you mean?" "She said, "When the president gets here, how does it work? You're secret service, right?" We laughed and said, "No, we were invited guests."

The rest of the party was great, and I met many significant people—including former President John Dramani Mahama. I even got a great picture with him and a signed copy of his book, *My First Coup D'etat*.

As we drove away, Frankie got an email apologizing for the delay: "I just cleared you for the party—you're good to go." I started laughing at the situation that had just unfolded. Technically, we had crashed the party. My adventures with Frankie continued to shape my early musical progress. These did not directly make me money, but they developed my confidence and presence. I was soaking in the energy of people at consistently higher success levels, which alone is priceless for growth.

Soon after, I had an opportunity to go to Dubai. This trip opened my mind to a new perspective. Initially, Frankie and I had planned to go to Afghanistan to interview the national soccer team. Everyone—and I mean everyone—said absolutely, "Don't go." Afghanistan was a war zone then, and the United States had many troops there fighting. So I decided not to go. I told the team my safety came first, and I couldn't risk my family not having a father.

Fortunately, the trip was changed to Dubai. I was now doing well in my real estate career and needed to tell a few clients that I needed to go to Dubai in the middle of some transactions. It was the merger of two opposing worlds. I remember telling a client whose home was in escrow that I would be leaving in two days, as I needed to attend some music-related events. It felt like I had just let someone in on my now big, hard-to-contain secret. He looked at me like he had no idea what to say—like I had unmasked something that didn't make sense.

It was a long flight—sixteen hours plus my layover in England—and things got interesting. The plane from England to Dubai had military types and contractors of various sorts on board. I sat next to a contractor who explained that he went to Afghanistan for about six months a year. I asked about his safety, and he said he wasn't fearful—that Americans were not targets. I couldn't believe that conversation. But what it did was open my mind. Times change, and conditions can get more serious. This was in 2016. In retrospect, I was gaining more worldwide perspectives. I was becoming increasingly comfortable with the unknown the world had to offer.

I thought back to how everyone told me not to go to Afghanistan, and then everyone said not to go to Mexico City because it's so dangerous. Then I got there. I realized Mexico City is one of the biggest cities in the world. There were and are dangerous parts, beautiful parts, and rich and poor areas. Mexico City was one of the most beautiful cities I have ever visited. I loved it. The food and architecture were remarkable—I would go there again in a heartbeat.

I started thinking this was another lesson in questioning the assumptions we have. We quickly use our sheltered information feed to draw conclusions on topics we know almost nothing about. Media can supply us with just bits—then we run that as the total. If we listened to this barrage, we would never go anywhere.

So there I was, touching down in Dubai. I always wanted to visit Dubai, and now I was there as a professional artist. I checked into one of the tallest hotels in Dubai, the Rose Rayhaan. Lying on my bed, I had a surreal realization in the stillness of where I was. I was now a comfortable international traveler.

I remember going to the hotel gym in my tank top and shorts. After a particularly intense workout, I was getting into the elevator. As the doors opened, I entered, dripping in sweat, and was face to face with three women in full-body burkas and their husbands. The women had only small eyeholes in the face portion to look out. All I could see was their eyes, and they had so much expression. There was an unspoken awkwardness in this long elevator ride of cultural collisions. It was a moment that helped me understand how different our two cultures are. Dubai was beautiful, futuristic in architecture, and unique. It helped me understand how other people live in the world. There is so much more than what we know and experience.

Frankie and I were treated like royalty. We were picked up in an ultra-luxury Mercedes and went to a jewelry store. There, the owner of the shop showed us a solid gold Quran. After that, we went to the top of the Burj Khalifa (the tallest building in the world at the time). The following day a driver drove us from our hotel in Dubai to have lunch in Abu Dhabi with the ambassador of Afghanistan. There were so many new and exciting things coming at me. My efforts at progress were paying off, and my value as an artist seemed to be ever-increasing.

The plan to have the soccer team come to Dubai and be interviewed fell through due to travel restrictions. We went to the headquarters of an Afghan airline, and the airline's head told us how safe it was for people to travel to and from Afghanistan. I was in awe. He explained who was in danger and who was very secure when traveling. He told us that attacks were long, organized events, and tourists were not the target. He went on to say how many people came and went safely every day. Hearing this perspective was very insightful to me. I'm not going into detail because the story's point is just this: Many times, things are not what we think they are. We are given very little information and believe that it is the truth. Yet, almost always, the truth is much more complicated. I instantly thought of the proverb with the simple but ever-truth-filled line, *the more we see, the less we know*. Many Americans are prejudiced and judgmental because of their lack of exposure. They would never feel such ill will if they traveled and saw the world. We are all susceptible to judgments and opinions based on distorted information. I try to always be adaptable in my views.

I felt like a changed man when I arrived back in San Jose. I had made a solo trip to the Middle East, having become a world traveler and then some. I had been exposed to new and different cultures and experiences. I was comfortable with my ever-evolving self and sensed no darkness lurking behind any corner. I was pushing forward and ready for whatever opportunity would come next.

Finding Purpose Through Pain

You will be emphatically warned against stepping out of your comfort zone by people who have never left theirs. You will be told places are dangerous by people who have never been there. You will be underestimated by people who have no clue about your talent level and how well-trained you are.

Break free of your own limitations and those put on you by others. Most people operate at headline-only depth and build entire belief systems on rumors and neighborhood wisdom.

Mexico City is beautiful, world-class city—many people told me not to go. All the "experts" had never been there. Nearly everyone told me not to go to Afghanistan; none of those people had been there. When I met an American who lived in Afghanistan for six months a year, everything changed. All the information from non-experts went out the window. We are quick to assume.

A studio engineer told me I couldn't punch in on a verse as fast as "Not a Game." He wasn't a rapper and didn't know my skill set. The list goes on. Trust your experience and gain real information from those who know, not headline historians and non-experts.

Don't let the ones who've never moved be the ones to tell you where not to go.

CHAPTER 16

FAST LANE

Mind numb and no sleep. Little raw and no defeat.
Lost and I find way, life in the fast lane.

"*Fast Lane*"

A conversation with Israel Rinaldo months prior kept running through my head. An open invitation to fly to Paris and record in one of the most sought-after studios was a rare opportunity. Having a place to stay for free was even better. I would just have to pay for my own food. It pushed me out of my comfort zone to even think of going on such an adventure. I decided I needed to be more comfortable being uncomfortable. So I went home and talked with Angela—we figured we could make it work. She would cover parenting and domestic duties when I was gone. I called Israel and let him know I was in. It was mid-October 2016.

Sitting alone in the San Jose airport, I tried to imagine what awaited me. I didn't have enough info on Israel to know what I was in for. All I knew was I needed to go—instinctually, it felt right. I wasn't even sure what Israel looked like, his age, or anything else. I had one picture he had posted online for reference. After the long overnight flight from San Jose to Orly Airport in Paris, I stood there, unsure of anything going forward. I realized Israel was much younger than me when he arrived with his friend Stephen in an old hatchback with a bumping subwoofer. He looked to be in his early twenties, thin with mid-length dreads. For a split second, I thought, *What the fuck am I doing? Was this a good idea? Am I living the wrong path?* We drove awkwardly out of the arrival terminal for two long minutes.

Then, all that faded when we turned on some music. Israel first played the new Young Thug song, "Wyclef Jean." I loved that song and had been playing it in the weeks leading up to my trip. The song's vibrations lifted the mood in the car as we all vibed to the tune. Once we connected over music, none of the other details mattered. We decided right there to make a song inspired by that tune. Less than five minutes in the car, our first idea was ready to go—time to create. Music bridged us. Music united us like so many others in this world. Music is the universal language that transcends race, age, nationality, and gender.

After sipping some wicked strong French Guiana rum, Israel and I started talking about life and music and how crazy it was to finally link in person. We drove around Paris in the early morning hours as we casually passed some of the world's best-known monuments. It was a perfect night to set the tone for the weeks ahead. Then it was just me. Lying on his couch alone in the stillness of the night, I became aware of what was ahead of me—pure madness. Fear crept over me momentarily—this was a lost, unknown road. I was really pushing forward. Then, like a flip of a switch, I embraced where I was and relaxed into the night.

I woke up a few hours later to Israel's roommate and girlfriend eating breakfast and watching TV, sitting on a folding chair a few feet from where I was sleeping in the living room. A few minutes later, Israel said, "Let's move, bro. We gotta meet Kwanz." I quickly downed a Nespresso shot, and we were out the door. We jumped on a bus without paying, then sneaked through the subway turnstile after a paying rider went through. Still half asleep when we hopped on the next bus, I said, "Bro, don't need to pay?"

Israel said, "He don't give a shit, bro . . . he just drives the bus." That was basically the vibe going forward. I wasn't just rolling through Paris—I was moving through it like the most "I don't give a shit" local you could find. This set the tone nicely, forcing me to quickly acclimate to my environment.

Just outside Versailles, we arrived at a beautiful lake where many people congregated—primarily male and female models. Local rapper Kwanz was having a photo shoot for his clothing company, and a small party was going on while people were waiting for their turn in front of the camera. Kwanz had me put on his new T-shirt, and the photographer took a fantastic photo for promotion with the castle of Versailles as my background.

From there, I found my way by bus over to the studio. It was called Studio Quai D'ivry—a place of music-making madness. It felt like an underground dungeon— music was being made twenty-four hours a day. It was gritty and perfect for music. I passed ten other studios on the way to Israel's, and I felt myself leveling up like you would before a big game as I walked. The swagger and vibe level were full tilt. Dancehall, Afrobeat, and hip-hop filled the smoky hallways as I rolled to a location deep in the trenches of the musical maze. I was ready to get on the mic when I arrived.

The air conditioner was out and it was hot as hell in Israel's studio, but somehow, that added to the madness.

I was pushing myself like crazy. The studio room Israel tracked in was owned by the famed DJ Phaxx. Although I didn't know of him, everyone kept telling me Phaxx was a huge deal. When I met him, we clicked. He was big and could intimidate people, but we saw eye to eye—you could tell he commanded respect.

I saw Phaxx put an unskilled rapper in his place. He brought a guy into the studio who said he could rhyme, so he gave him a chance. In the booth, the guy sounded like a bit of a clown, so Phaxx ended the charade. He told him in French to get out of the vocal booth, and when he got back to the control room, he asked why the fuck he was wasting his time. He asked me, in front of this guy, what I thought. I told him I just came halfway across the world, and every time I step in the booth, I don't play. He loved that. I think we really linked at that moment. Ever since that moment, I've adopted a phrase, "Get out of the booth," and I use it if someone isn't bringing high-level vocals. The honesty of that is amazing. Thankfully, I've never been told to get out of the booth.

We were at the studio laying down scratch tracks for a few hours, and then around 1:00 a.m., Israel had a session with some Italian rappers who had just arrived to track a few songs. After they entered the studio, I had a weak moment—I was exhausted. I had barely slept for four days, and Israel was a madman on all-night sessions. At about 2:00 a.m., the studio had fifteen people working on a session, standing room only. It was too much. I went to a park by the studio and lay on a bench. I felt alone and vulnerable. Then I called Angela and said I didn't know if I could do this. She said, "Just go all in and enjoy it. It will be over soon." So I did. I went to the store, bought a bottle of wine, and decided I was all in.

We slept in the studio that night. There was still no air conditioner, and the couches were so dirty that you wouldn't ever think of sleeping on them unless you were completely gassed. It was like 100 degrees. At about 6:00 a.m., the musicians arrived to record a song. I slapped contacts in my eyes with a dirty, sweaty finger, felt the burn, downed some vitamins with some trail mix, and then we started to create a reggae song based on our liking of the Wyclef track. A few hours later, the instrumental music was done. I then laid down the lyrics and wrote a decent chorus. I was inspired creatively, and the words I spoke into the mic came somewhat effortlessly due to this new inspiration.

That night, we went to a nightclub where Israel worked—one of the premier lounges in Paris—and I helped with the sound. It was very upscale. Looking back, this was an extraordinary moment. There were no tourists here, just great Parisian energy, and I was a part of it. These are the little perks that I find tremendous value in. It had a relaxed, artistic vibe—dim light and red velvet seats.

After working sound at the nightclub, we went over to the gardens at the Louvre, and at about 4:00 a.m., we decided to return to the studio. I laid the chorus of "Fast Lane" just before sunrise. I was on no sleep, somewhat drunk, and still ready to work. I sang the lyrics "raw, no sleep, raw, defeat, lost way . . ." in the studio's control room to Israel, and he said "no." I decided to show him anyway, went into the booth, laid it, and he said it was perfect.

On we went. It was like this for three weeks. I would go to sleep after sunrise, wake up at 10:00 a.m., run around with a camera crew led by a young, talented filmmaker named James, record in the studio, and then drive home as the sun rose.

Somehow, I was driving the group—without an international license. I guess that was because Israel didn't drive. We were six deep in a little car going over to the studio. Dancehall and hip-hop music played. I felt a look from the car next to me, a look of hate and disproval, not at me but at the whole vehicle. It was then that I realized the feeling of actual racism. That feeling of making someone feel like they didn't belong. Almost everyone I was with in Paris had roots in Africa. Everyone was dark-skinned, a new perspective for me as the only light-skinned person in the group. It helped me understand the awful, deep-seated racial experience that people go through. I was able to see more clearly what life was like in another's shoes.

I also grew my perspective on different cultures. That car was filled with people treating me with the warmest of welcomes. I carried a new appreciation for looking beyond skin color. I hope for a day when skin color matters as much as the color of one's eyes or hair, as the legendary Bob Marley once said in a song.

As we kept going toward the studio, I was driving like we do in California—after stopping, turning right on a red light. They didn't understand why I kept going right on red lights. I told them it was because we do that in California. They looked at me like we were lawless outlaws. That was a great moment—especially since Israel was the last person I thought would be concerned about my driving. It helped me understand the little variations cultures have and how fun it is to find them.

I kept my hidden identity as a realtor to myself on the nearly month-long trip. I would escape from time to time into my "invisible phone booth" to switch to the realtor hat and answer some emails and things for my clients. Then, back into the vocal booth, I switched back to the artist and entered the music world. The only one who seemed to notice my other life was James, the filmmaker, who was very inquisitive about my story, but I brushed it off. This life of hidden identity was tiring. I didn't like having these two worlds, but they don't blend perfectly. I would gloss over how I made a living while making music and dismiss the significance of my music career to my clients, telling people, "I make music in my free time." The correct wording is, "I push forward music every day of my life with a never-dimming fire inside to create and become the best artist I can be." Describing my music as a hobby would be the furthest thing from the truth. It's my escape, how I cope with the world, and ultimately what gives me purpose.

Israel told me we would pick up a rapper from the train station. He was coming in from the south of France, and his name was Vödoo. He got in and seemed cool but flustered by the trip. He was Haitian French and had an intense 1990s lyrical hip-hop vibe—somewhere between Guru and 2Pac for my hip-hop heads. He also seemed close to my age—it was cool to feel like I wasn't a decade older than everyone. Also, we were both strangers in this land. We were lyricists who converged in Paris, and it was time to make music.

Israel, Vödoo, and I went to eat at the housing projects near the studio. They had a fantastic dish called *yassa* that was only a few euros, but so good. Going into the building, people were cooking corn in shopping carts—creating a makeshift grill by putting hot coals in a metal bucket and using a part of the cart as the grill. When the main restaurant was closed, we went to the apartment of someone who had prepared something in the room. It was so cool to me. It was so different from anything I had seen but felt so real. It felt more awkward to roll into one of those hipster coffee houses than to roll into here.

After lunch, we returned to the studio and started working on a tune. We decided it should be about how music was our life, and we started working on the instrumental, then the lyrics. Instantly, I found a hook, and we got to work.

> *And I never chill, filled with the harmony. Still makes me ill. Lay the beat fill and the bass then I go, this is all that I know, and the studio is my home, with this mic that I own. And music is inside me, where you'll always find me. Rhythm in my soul, and I never gonna slow down.*
>
> *"Ma Musique" feat. Vödoo*

After we put down the song, Vödoo, Stephen, and I returned to Israel's. Israel stayed at the studio to track another artist. We were chilling on the couch, watching hypnotic dancehall videos past midnight, when Vödoo asked me how old I was. I said, "Thirty-seven as of today. It is my birthday." The look he gave me was intense. Like I was playing a trick on him. He said, "Oh, you mean the nineteenth?" I said, "No, the eighteenth"—since it was already 2:00 a.m. and I had forgotten it was now the next day. He said, "Are you fucking with me? My birthday is also the eighteenth." We instantly whipped out our ID cards because we were in disbelief about the whole thing. Sure enough, he and I recorded a song together on our birthdays without anyone knowing it.

As the trip drew to a close, we agreed to stay awake that night and charge through until morning on the last day. We finished the rum, and James drove us to Orly Airport. I said goodbye to Vödoo and Israel as James filmed the departure. I decompressed on a bench outside my flight terminal before my 11:00 a.m. takeoff. Everything ran through my head as I experienced my first moment of silence in three weeks. It was great. I felt my body relax from the weeks of that fast-paced life as I prepared to reenter the domestic world awaiting me at home.

Finding Purpose Through Pain

You don't always need all the details to take the next step, but you do need guts. Let your instinct lead, as waiting for the perfect clarity for your next move will leave you with no move at all. I flew to Paris not knowing what I'd find, or who I'd meet, or how any of it would turn out. If you want a deeper life, stop waiting for full confidence, safety, or assurance. Send the message. Book the trip and get on the damn plane. You will be changed for the better because of it.

Make sure you go somewhere that shakes you. Growth isn't just in meditation, therapy, and self-help books. Paris shaped me because it was wild, unscripted, and very raw. That's where identity can be shaped for you. It's in those places that unsettle your rhythm and comfort. If you have spent too long in a routine, go somewhere that gives you none of the things you are familiar with. Life can shake you awake and give you a new appreciation for what is out there in the world to experience.

Sometimes the most important thing is to just stay in it. It won't always feel inspiring or exciting. It won't always be quite right. You could be exhausted, homesick, and doubting your talents and skill set. Stay in it; those moments of potential quitting are where the shift happens. I assure you, if you don't run, you will change. If you don't fold, you will rise.

CHAPTER 17

BRIGHTER DAYS

Man, I take own road, embrace unknown. Life in phone trying to maintain home. Vultures swarm and they try to harm, I can really take it all. And jab and sprawl work through the pain. Push through walls and form my lane, and break of shame vision remains show no restrain, no time to gain.

"The Unknown Roads"

I WAS OFF TO Miami three weeks later for a studio session at Velvet Basement. When I landed in Miami, Tony and Carlos picked me up at the airport. They were a production team out of Venezuela and were in Miami to build their company, Polaris Studios. They had also found me on social media and wanted to meet in person after a few remixes to produce an EP.

Again, I got off the plane and greeted people I had never met. They were about my age and were family men. They didn't drink or smoke; there was something almost mathematical and detailed about them. We stayed in a penthouse apartment at the top of a high-rise in downtown Miami, overlooking the water and the arena where the Miami Heat play basketball. On the night before recording, I sat in my room in a high-rise overlooking the shores of Miami. I was now so far from where I had started that it brought tears to my eyes. The scared little boy was gone. In the stillness now, I felt comfort. I had leveled up once again.

The following day, we fired up the Bialetti coffee maker and headed to the studio in a no-nonsense fashion. We arrived at the Velvet Basement, a good-sized studio with an excellent control room and one of my favorite mics set up—the Neumann M 149. With the owner, Robert Dante, at the mixing board, which was previously the control board of the *Tonight Show* in New York City prior to him purchasing it—we got into the first song, "The Unknown Roads." We were recreating "Unknown Road" but gave it its own unique title. When I started singing, the lyrics didn't feel right. They were dull and forced. We were trying to duplicate what I did on "Unknown Road," and I realized we needed to change the cadence of the vocal to fit in the pocket of what Tony and Carlos had done musically. So I sang a new verse, and the track came alive with its own identity. But I didn't have the lyrics entirely written out, so I used the power of the moment. I freestyled much of it, with musicians and engineers listening to my every word and pitch. After Paris, though, this wasn't uncomfortable for me. I was able to go into the space I knew so well. I could find my world within the music, like at home in my basement.

We knocked out four tunes before making "Hate Over Love?" on the spot with our extra studio time. I freestyled—also known as improvised singing—my way through the tune.

I felt different as I sat in the airport after the session on my way home. Now a grown man on a mission, I could stand behind the mic in a professional studio, with a control room full of near strangers, and improvise from the gut—no script, no mask, just mastery earned through years in the shadows. I was no longer chasing permission—I was claiming space. I learned that being great isn't just about talent—it's about being ready when the RECORD button turns red. And this applies to all aspects of life.

We decided to call the EP *Brighter Days.* Carlos and Tony mixed and mastered it in Miami, and I was just waiting to get the finished product. A few months prior, Israel had connected me to the owner of Rebel Sound Records, Zack Reed. Zack used to be in marketing and A&R for VP Records and then started his reggae label, Rebel Sound, after leaving VP. Instinctually, I knew I wanted to work with him. I always wanted to be on a record label, and this felt like my chance to make it happen. Once I got the finished album in hand, I sent it to Zack to see what he thought—anxiously awaiting his response. Zack loved it and said he would happily release the *Brighter Days* EP.

Now, I had distribution through Sony Music's the Orchard, and was on a reggae label, Rebel Sound Records. I also had a growing number of highly talented musicians who had my back, which took me to the next level. As I was always looking for increased momentum, this milestone helped propel me forward.

I'd found a place where my music fit and a tribe I belonged to. Zack knew many of the artists I listened to personally, and it was exciting to start getting plugged into the artery of reggae. He had a label with music from Common Kings, Meta and the Cornerstones, E.N Young (Tribal Seeds), Yami Bolo, and many more. I felt so grateful for Zack, his belief in me, and the connections to the music industry I loved.

I asked Zack if he had any dancehall-type riddims. I had always loved dancehall as lyrical music that delivers potent verses. He sent me a riddim by DJ JFX, a prominent reggae DJ who had worked with Half Pint and Sister Carol. This was a proper dancehall tune, with lots of space for the vocals to fit. This song became known as "Turn It On."

When I submitted the song's final versions, Zack asked who mixed and mastered it. I told him it was me. He had no idea that I had this skill set. I explained that I went to sound engineering school and always wanted complete control of my music's sound. With that, he started sending me reggae music to mix and master. I began working on mixes for known artists throughout the reggae and dancehall scene. I set aside a small block of time each day to mix other artists' music, improving my engineering skills and earning some money as I went.

Music and life are all about climbing up the ladder a little bit every day—slowly moving through the ranks toward greatness. I've learned that other musicians or high-level people in any category know who has "it" and who doesn't. It is that thing you can't describe other than a level of authenticity and uniqueness that sets some people apart from everyone except the best in the field. I cherish climbing the ladder of validation. I also get motivated by those who think I don't possess "it."

I voiced on E.N Young's *Raggamuffin Ride Riddim* album on a collaboration tune with Craigy-T of the reggae group T.O.K. This was a new opportunity to be on the album and collaborate with a big name in the reggae scene. The song "Cease and Settle" differed significantly from the original version. E.N had taken mostly Craig's lyrics and took off half of mine. Did this sting? Yep. Did I understand why? Yep. Craigy-T brought "it" on the verses. He came with a significant presence and flow. I needed to let my pride go and understand that as an artistic decision, it was the right one. With "Cease and Settle," I learned that sometimes the betterment of the art requires some compromise that can be difficult. Craigy brought more "it" to the table. I needed to level up.

Finding Purpose Through Pain

Be willing to step into the unknown. Real growth begins when the comfort ends. Traveling solo, trusting in strangers, and adapting on the fly allows powerful breakthroughs in art, work, and life. If you spend time building skills, then you will be ready when the opportunity calls.

You won't always feel prepared. Being great isn't just about talent—it's about being willing and stepping into the booth and giving everything you have when the RECORD button turns red, in any aspect of life.

As you level up, you'll find yourself in rooms where others are more seasoned and skilled. Let these moments humble you, but don't shrink. They are proof that you're climbing and getting closer. Use them as fuel. Put your long-term mission above your ego.

CHAPTER 18

WASN'T ME

They hoped and predicted that I'd get convicted. They said too explicit, my dreams are too vivid. I pushing my limit, and everything give it, and they are too crooked, I flow like a liquid.

"Wasn't Me"

In my mid-twenties, I began to doubt my abilities. The positive reinforcement wasn't there. The inner critic had to be stifled so the fire inside could burn bright again. Thankfully, now my moments of weakness get overridden by some call, text, email, or notification at the right time to snap me out of it and give me momentum. An opportunity will present itself whenever I have an "Am I good enough at this?" moment. When I relax, push forward, and give the slightest thought to surrender, I bounce back stronger. A decade before, it was a feeling of desperation. I wasn't sharing the music I made, doing shows, or engaging in life. People started doubting me.

Some "friends" saw a wounded man and thought this was who I was—all I would become. They thought they saw someone who never pushed to see what he could do. Well over a decade away from that stage in my life, I now feel pride. They were wrong. The memories of the darkest times fade as I look around at who I now talk with and what I do daily. I was inspired to tell them they were wrong. At twenty-seven, I was far from being washed up and bowing out—it was just a low moment in my life.

I had been hearing from others that time was running out since I was around twenty-seven. Perpetually, this expiration date kept getting pulled back further in my own mind until I developed a drastically different approach to this whole age and entertainment thing. It was this: I am an artist. Just like a painter. People don't care about the age of a painter, so why the fuck does the age of a musical artist matter? It's never too late to pursue your dreams.

Some people didn't support my music or my real estate career. They didn't think I had what it took to thrive in life. They did a character assessment while I was in my darkest moments and thought that was me. They thought the most wounded Ben was the best I could do. I wanted to call all those who doubted me and tell them what I was doing now. I wrote a song called "Wasn't Me," inspired by the doubters of the past. It was about everyone who told me I'd never make it—the people who said I was too fat and lazy.

The trauma and wounds from the past emerge when I'm in a weak space or around negative people. That's when the doubts of the past tend to reveal themselves again. I become embarrassed by the scars. This is when the burns and bruises show themselves. When I think I'm less-than. When I resort back to thinking, I'm still in the shadows.

So, I don't hang around negativity. Period. Whether family, old friends, people I encounter at my kids' schools, or whomever, I move on if it's not positive push-forward stuff—end of story. After I hang out with a toxic individual, I feel shittier than before the interaction. Becoming aware of your mental state before and after dealing with someone will give you an answer if they are healthy or not in your life—act accordingly.

Sometimes your gut instinct gets derailed by people with power and fame. They talk so grand and stand so tall. They develop confidence and strength. Sometimes, the feeling that something is off with someone gets pushed down because of all they offer and promise. I've had that happen many times, but sometimes it's too huge of an opportunity to understand how big a deception you face. I'm as guilty as anyone of disregarding my judgment and chasing after broken promises.

Quick story with a lesson: I met an artist manager—let's call him Louie. I hadn't heard of him, but I did see his resume. It was a little abstract but listed the names of the best in entertainment. He said he liked my music and was into it. Louie asked me to head to LA to meet with him. I took the seven-hour bus ride to mentally transition from my domestic life to that of a musician—I like to give myself the space to enter that world before arriving.

The double-decker Megabus started on its journey. I sat next to Nate, a curly-haired guy carrying a huge item that looked like a rolled-up carpet. After introducing himself, he explained it was a canvas painting he had picked up from the restaurant where it was displayed. Not just any painting. It was made by having a woman lie naked on a canvas, then he poured wine on her and let it dry and imprint on the canvas. He showed me a pic of the canvas and the imprint of the sexy nude woman the dried wine made. It's a genius idea, in my opinion.

The painting startled a few guests at the restaurant, so Nate wanted to come and find a better home for it. After hearing his story, I was sold on Nate's authenticity. We discussed music and life throughout the ride, reminiscent of the movie *Fear and Loathing in Las Vegas*. Nate had extensive experience traveling the world and interviewing bands. He provided me with valuable insights into marketing techniques through Hype Machine and SubmitHub. Those proved to be useful tools down the road. Beyond that, Nate had the type of joy and enthusiasm for life I felt had dimmed in me. Life was to be lived to the fullest—even while on a bus ride to LA. I loved it.

I met with Louie in Los Angeles and discussed finalizing his management of my music career. I had progressed far enough as an artist to attract interest from people in the inner circle of the industry. We planned a tour. I brought in Zack and artists from the label. We laid out the whole route, and I arranged with my family to be gone for a month and a half on the tour. I put aside real estate to focus on prepping for the tour.

It didn't pan out. It was an untruth that Louie told, and it just kept going. Somewhere along the line, Louie knew he couldn't put it together and didn't tell anyone. He let it go on until I reached out personally to the supposed headliner and found out he wasn't aware of the tour or Louie. I busted the lie. It was humiliating to tell everyone what happened, but it wasn't the only time—just the most significant.

I've had plenty of times like that. I've had meetings and verbal and written deals with international music managers at the Beverly Hills Hotel that didn't pan out. I've had drinks with a former NFL player and discussed playing at a Caribbean music festival that didn't pan out. I've rolled—in a Maserati—to private clubs to discuss collaborations that didn't pan out.

These times when things don't line up, give appreciation for those things that do. It helps to remind myself of those who have my back. Not all people in music are like that. When I find one of the true ones, I stay linked to them. Too many people just don't have steady, solid roots.

Alone on a bus heading back to San Jose from LA, I was very introspective, thinking about how much of the entertainment business is hype. So many promises and projects don't pan out. I contemplated how many agreements are fraudulent and how many people talk big and act overconfident. I gazed out the window at the landscape void of anything but tumbleweeds—Highway 5 gives you plenty of time to think.

I pictured myself walking in the Santa Cruz Mountains I knew so well. As I walked, I looked around at some trees as tall as the redwoods. Some seemed off—they weren't quite right. Yes, they were tall—most of the trees around them were dwarfed in comparison—but there was a problem. They were so concerned about growing that they didn't take the time to grow roots and strong trunks. They had no foundation or strength. One by one, these trees came crashing down all around me. Those who faked their way to the top dropped. This is life. Growth—like a redwood—takes time. You need to sustain through trauma.

You need to build slowly, with a solid foundation. You need to embrace your scars, not run from them. You must be stable to last in the music business—and the forest. Many people in entertainment are like tall trees with no roots. They are unstable, so they come falling down—full of lies and built upon a foundation of deceit.

> *And they pulling us down, and we try to climb. Show me how life shouldn't be, no hide. Coward with lies, and they pull those teeth. Smiles inside, but I cannot breathe. Loving my life, so they can't be me. My eyes open, and they can't see. I find they fake, they the enemy. Chopping them down like a falling tree . . . something in the air just don't feel right, and then a few of these trees falling down tonight.*
>
> *"Falling Trees"*

I have also realized that when people know influential people, it doesn't mean they, too, have power. Someone can be in the room while something epic is being done musically. They can have the pictures in the studio with a famous artist and be at dinner afterward. They can tell the stories and factually back them up. But it doesn't mean they did anything. It doesn't mean an artist would ever work with them. Being Mick Jagger's best friend doesn't mean he'd put you on a track. It doesn't mean he'd vouch for you and connect you with his contact list. It means you can be in the studio on the couch when they are recording—and be happy you got that.

People cling to influential acquaintances and talk about how well they know them. People promise and don't deliver—toying with the hopes and dreams of those trying to make it. People talk big and stand tall, like large trees with no roots. The music business is the land of falling trees.

Finding Purpose Through Pain

People may judge you based on your weakest moments, crystallizing who they think you are at your rock bottom. You are not your lowest point. With time, growth, and dedication, you can climb so far above it that those same people's judgment becomes irrelevant.

Some people will look and talk powerfully but have no roots. A nice car, confidence, and a bunch of name-dropping don't equal integrity. Life is full of tall trees with shallow roots—people who try to cheat or inauthentically climb without putting in the time. Beware of those who promise a lot but deliver little to nothing. Trust in your gut through the smoke screen of hype.

The best growth is steady, rooted, and resilient. Remember the redwood trees and the years it takes them to develop a foundation that allows them to stand for centuries. There are no shortcuts worth taking—give things time, endure pain, and have patience.

CHAPTER 19

ALL OK

Just don't slip away, I'm living for today, I'm living through this pain, I'm pushing out the shade.

"All OK"

I WAS HAVING LUNCH with my pops around the corner from my house, feeling a little discouraged from all the false promises I had experienced in the music industry, when I got a DM from DJ Power. I had met Power at a studio session in LA a few months prior. Power's work ethic was notable. He was focused, there to work. You could tell that he was about the music.

I was shocked he was coming to me directly. I hadn't talked to him since that night at the studio, but we had a mutual friend who connected us. He said I could perform with him at his Las Vegas residency at Sapphire Pool Party. We would be there for two weeks—another long stretch to be gone. Angela was supportive, as always, about my next musical adventure. She helped me line everything up, even helping to book the flight. With that, my music momentum sparked back up.

It is worth noting how important a supportive spouse is. When someone understands you, life is open. Within my marriage, I have never felt trapped. I have never felt like I couldn't live the life I wanted. There has always been an understanding of the other person and what they want from life. For me, music is vital. It allows me to have some great adventures. Angela supports that. Sometimes, I hear people comment that their wives would "never let them go" to the places I go. Why? Are they some deranged child who, when left alone, can't care for themselves and show restraint?

I landed in Vegas in late July 2019, and the temperature read 110 degrees. It was the night of the Manny Pacquiao vs. Keith Thurman fight at the MGM Grand, so the casino was packed. People dressed their best, and celebrity-level people were everywhere—this was another level of energy.

The limo arrived the next day to pick up Power and me outside the front lobby of the casino. As we drove, I saw the club in the distance—it was the size of a Costco. We got out, walked past the Lamborghinis, Bentleys, and other luxury cars, gave a handshake to the six bouncers, and got our all-access badges. We went past the main pool and then up to the VIP pool next to the DJ booth. As I settled into the private cabana, I felt that I was in a strange world, with my picture and name on the large posters greeting guests throughout the club. I was three months from turning forty, and I was an ambassador in the land of reckless and uninhibited. How crazy it was, and I had no one I knew there to nudge and grin with. This was not my scene. This was not a reggae club—but somehow, I had become a featured artist here. My face was staring back at me from the poster directly in front of me.

This first show at the Sapphire felt like a rite of passage to another level of musicianship and life adaptability. Performing is about courage and dedication to craft. It's about handling it and then enjoying the feeling of accomplishment. The gold is in crafting the song, prep, and emotions before and after. Performing is a unique place where I connect with a large group of people with lyrics I made in the most private settings.

After the show, in the hotel room the next day, I witnessed the intense work ethic of a top-level DJ. I would vibe with Power as he searched for hours for the songs for the next show, constantly clicking through music and checking the selected songs in sequence. You could hear him practicing from way down the hall, getting out of the elevator. The sounds of dancehall and Afrobeat filled the hallway for all guests on our floor. Power didn't care. He was all about listening loud, mimicking the levels at a club. He wanted to feel how the music would feel when performing.

DJ Power was older than me but worked harder than most and didn't come off as aging. My narrative of what I "should" be doing was deceptive. I was afraid as my fortieth birthday approached—this was an end to an era. I had always thought forty was when life needed to shift—only I felt no change inside. There is no expiration date to that which gives me purpose and satisfaction. I'm not making art for the chance of being famous. I make music because it is me. Music gets me through the struggles and close to peace.

Life too strained but a so I ride, got God inside,
friend by my side.
Brethren ride, and we combine, got a stronger mind,
I working toward the prize.
Deal that I sign on the dotted line, no backing out
full throttle ride.
Doubt chasing, clout racing, time that a racing, hard
to break in.

"Close 2 Peace" feat. Craigy-T

After my last show at the Sapphire, I sat comfortably in the VIP pool overlooking the venue with a drink in my hand, reflecting on how different my life was and how sound my space was. As a thirty-nine-year-old married father of two, I had pushed myself out of my comfort zone. I was a touring musician and recording artist. I wore many hats, and this moment in the VIP spa greatly reflected how far I had come over the last decade. I'd lived free—my soul was not tormented with anxiety and regrets. I thought about the intensity and uniqueness of the journey. The feeling was like being in Paris, Miami, Mexico City, Dubai, or NYC airports. I had a sense that I was reaching closer to the real me. I was growing and becoming comfortable wherever I went and whatever I was doing.

I returned from Las Vegas at the end of the summer of 2019. Kendo was working at the same local motorcycle dealership (GP Sports) that I had worked at in high school. Gianna was off school for the summer, and Angela was in Nashville with her friends.

On a Friday morning, I woke up to Gianna running down the hallway into my bedroom. By the sound of her steps, I could tell something was different. "It's raining in your studio!" Gianna called out. Confused, I ran downstairs to witness a downpour on my entire musical life. My monitors, computer, desk, mics—memorabilia from years of shows—were soaked and ruined. The Sheetrock on the ceiling was peeling off. I stood in a few inches of standing water on the soaked carpet, and as Kendo and Gianna looked on from the staircase, I let out a helpless "Noooo!" My past flooded my mind as water dripped down on me.

Slushing through the water, I quickly started disconnecting everything and got shocked as I reached to unplug the computer. Working at lightning speed, I moved my sensitive, soaked electrical equipment to the dining room to dry out. I put metal buckets on the ground to collect the falling water, and the pinging sound was constant for over twenty-four hours as the water settled. I soaked up water in a five-gallon shop vacuum for the next two days, trying to dry the carpet. I tried to dry the floor and the walls with every fan I had. I even tried to paint the stained studio walls with Gianna to distract myself from the significance of the situation. I couldn't bring myself to admit what was inevitable. Fire, earthquake, and now a flood in my sacred place of safety? Finally, I started to realize this was more than I could handle. Reality set in. I told Angela we had better call insurance—the studio was officially closed.

I discovered that the refrigerator's water line had burst, and water had poured onto my kitchen floor like an open faucet for over eight hours while we slept. The water seeped into the floor and slowly created the rainstorm I witnessed that morning. We had a flood remediation company come over, and they demolished our kitchen, laundry room, and my entire music studio—nothing left but concrete walls and two-by-four studs. They isolated all the rooms with plastic and had multiple large heat fans running for days. Our house was in quarantine.

I sat at my dining room table, staring at my broken-down Pro Tools rig and numerous boxes stacked high around me. I realized it would be a long time before I had my space back. My computer was jacked, the mic ruined, and I was not cooking up a gem anytime soon. My room to create would be gone for a while. This brought me back to my youth—the same way I had felt when our homes were destroyed by fire and earthquake. More than that, the place that gave me my identity and grounded me during life's difficulties had been taken. I lost the outlet, escape, and refuge I'd had for nearly twenty years—my music studio.

The pull to create and immerse myself in my music has only increased with age. While most of my peers had long since given up on a music career, I have become more compelled daily to progress. I rarely watch sports other than basketball and don't like wasting much time chilling. Yet there is a powerful, intense, constantly increasing feeling inside me to create. There is something I'm searching for, and I'm confident that the search is endless, always trying to get closer to the source of creation in art and life. There is a truth somewhere in the music that is most pure and closest to the universal energy. I feel closest to God—whatever you idealize that to be—when I connect into the creative flow. It is my church and one I want to return to daily until I leave this planet. When I lost the studio and had nowhere to create, I lost some of my identity and felt incomplete.

I started revisiting unfinished Pro Tools sessions. I didn't have a studio, but I could contact musicians to help me finish my incomplete songs. I had a draft of a tune with Ras Fraser Jr. and Bobby Hustle, but the drums weren't done yet. I had Dan Konopka from OK Go lace the drums and Tony from the "Better Days" Miami session on bass.

Lyrically, I was speaking of that feeling that my identity was slipping away because I couldn't make music. I was singing about losing my sense of worth, needing to step back, and realizing everything would be okay. I was starting to feel my vibrance slip away with every passing day. I was losing that excitement for life that had grown so familiar.

We still had no kitchen, and eating out for every meal had lost its charm. I had no studio, and walking past the unused musical equipment was torturous. I grabbed a seat in my grandfather's rocking chair. The chair I had known my whole life had been a staple in my studio for twenty years. It was now next to the boxes and broken gear. I thought of my grandfather and how far my life had come since he was around. Gone were the days of my youth—innocent and free. Life was complicated, and days were zooming by. I was eight days from forty years old and kept thinking about how proud my grandfather would have been of the man I had become. The thought of him returned a sense of kindness and love to me. To remember that voice of stability was what I needed. I felt guided. All was OK.

Finding Purpose Through Pain

Stay ready because you never know when a breakthrough might come. Momentum can return in an instant and often does. It only takes one call or message to turn things around. When you stay committed to progress and keep sharp, that next step can show up when you least expect it.

Age has nothing to do with climbing in life. For many years, I thought it did. There is no expiration date on living with purpose and passion. If you allow it to, the inner fire can burn brighter with age, not dimmer. Remember that there is no stopping or aging out of that which gives you purpose and satisfaction. There will always be a lane to connect to it. It might change, due to the physical limitations age can contain in some fields, but there will always be a channel available to continue with that which you love.

Our setbacks are our tests. When your space gets taken away or destroyed, it shakes your identity. These can be reminders that our environments are fragile. We must always be ready to rebuild and push forward with resilience. When I lost my studio, I gave in to the chaos for a while. That void of not creating helped me to realize how important it was and never to be taken for granted.

Performing in Las Vegas at that club might not have been how I imagined it going. But what it did do was let me reflect on how far I have come and that I was adaptable and prepared to take any opportunity given to me, no matter how uncomfortable. I was going to show up.

I encourage you to keep showing up—keep climbing. The path might not be predictable. Embrace the detours and create in the chaos.

CHAPTER 20

SOUL

You gotta push the fear away. I, don't care what they say, yeah, don't hang with no fakes. I, trying to make it great. So, world in front of me. I, trying to raise these beings. I, trying to paint these scenes. I, live a life extreme.

"Soul"

MONTHS PASSED, AND MY dining room looked like a storage facility, containing all the remnants of our kitchen, laundry room, and music studio. Dust was piling up on the equipment and mics that I still had. Finally, after many months, insurance was ready to pay for my damaged gear, and I was excited to create a new, better rig.

I visited a local computer store and had them build a custom PC that would be capable of everything I could throw at it in music creation. Technology would no longer be a limitation. I bought a new mic and audio interface, then I set up the computer in my dining room, clearing out space in between all the other items.

I didn't have my studio, but now I had my audio rig. As I loaded the first Pro Tools session up, surrounded by boxes, it felt like I was returning home. I worked with a new appreciation for music and its creation, and quickly made a riddim from scratch. Then I was ready. I flipped on the new mic and went to work. I realized how quickly the dexterity of vocals deteriorates when not in daily use—I had to re-find my voice's authenticity. I was recording with my headphones on, singing loudly in my dining room as Angela and Gianna walked by and continued with domestic duties. It didn't matter to me, though, since I was back. I had Gianna say one word, "road," at the beginning of the tune and flipped a delay on it, so it rolled into the lyrics of what became "Rolling Stone." I had so much focus despite the chaos. It might have been in my dining room with all its distractions, but I was able to get my identity back and speak my truth.

> *Where you wanna be?, Where you wanna go? Do you know your goal? Do you know your day?, How you wanna dress? How you playing chess? What's your next move? What you gotta do? Heal and rest? How you pass the test when you barely sleep?*
>
> *"Rolling Stone"*

Since I was a kid, I always fought against losing creative relevancy. I never wanted to become the guy in the hairband and leather jacket who was stuck in a time capsule. Someone out of touch and holding on to something that was no longer meaningful. That was the image that worked for me, at least. I never wanted to be stuck in any timeframe that wasn't the present. I was and am determined to be an ever-evolving artist. I never want to be known for one thing or style, especially trendy things. They leave you behind as the world turns. I always try to make genuine and timeless music that people connect with.

Moments of significant change remind me of the speed of life. Kendo was trying to figure out where his life would take him. He was now preparing his college entrance essays, and I was helping him come up with effective content. His unusual path emerged as we brainstormed significant accomplishments. He courageously faced open heart surgery and became a 400-meter sprinter. At fifteen, he worked at my friend's market. He took a two-hour train alone from San Jose to Stockton every Sunday. He took a college course on astronomy during his junior year in high school, which required him to drive alone to the Southern California desert right after getting his driver's license. He went to a NASA space camp in Alabama and wanted to be an astronaut. He dealt with having a jaw wired shut after he fell off a skateboard, missed school, and got straight-A grades while having to teach himself from home. That skateboard fall changed his life. He realized who his friends were and weren't. He prioritized what mattered from there, focusing on academics at the highest level. I was proud of my son.

As Kendo wrote his college entrance essays, I sat beside him and proudly thought back on the difficulties and sacrifices I had made to stay in his life eighteen years prior. The decision to spend over five hours every Friday in a car driving to pick him up was hard, but long after the toll of driving disappeared, the fond memories remained.

The memories of the car rides span from his earliest days to the last time I drove to Lodi to pick him up from high school. His whole childhood, until he turned sixteen, was framed in those drives every Friday. We were together in that car during the infant car seat phase until the day we took our final two-hour trip home, closing the door on his adolescence. I am grateful that I no longer have the grueling rides but miss the time with him. A time when the only thing to do was talk. Now, we wave goodbye from the front porch and watch his car fade into the distance.

There are moments in life that don't announce themselves with a dramatic entrance but shift everything. For me, it was a quiet morning—December 4, 2019. I picked up my Kindle and started reading. That small act, that seemingly ordinary choice, changed my life. The first book? *30 Days: Change Your Habits, Change Your Life* by Marc Reklau—a fitting title. The words weren't complex, but they hit deep. They met me exactly where I was—stuck, scattered, searching—and gave me motivation. I didn't know it then, but I had just walked through a new door.

With my music studio unavailable, I needed a new outlet. That first reading session gave me something unexpected: clarity—a spark. The next morning, I found myself craving that same stillness. Coffee in hand, Kindle glowing in the predawn hours, I was suddenly rewiring my brain one page at a time. I felt sharper. More focused. More *me*. Since that day, I haven't stopped. Reading became my daily mental workout, averaging seventy-five books a year, with the rare exception of a day when I wake up later than planned. It's one of the things I've done with total consistency, and it restructured the way I think, act, and live. That one decision didn't just change my habits—it gave me back my mind.

Most of my progress in life can be traced back to the fundamentals of my weightlifting—getting a little bit better every day. With weightlifting, muscles grow, you get stronger, you look better, and your inner happiness grows. With reading, the mind sharpens, you learn, you feel better, and internal happiness increases. It's no exaggeration to say the neurological pathways become more fluid through reading—like the feeling of muscle growth or cardiovascular conditioning in running. With reading, I could combine all the things I love and learn about daily. Books on self-improvement, motivation, health, fitness, relationships, music, and much more started to improve all aspects of my life. I gained extensive knowledge on an incredible catalog of subjects that interested me. I started reading every morning and night without exception. Reading became another anchor, like music and fitness—a mandatory part of my daily regimen. I can't overstate this fact—daily reading changed my life.

Through self-help books, I reframed my view of the past. Instead of holding on to the "poor me," I discovered positive lessons from my past experiences. The fire brought about a brand-new house. That new house destroyed in an earthquake brought about living in a fantastic home. In retrospect, the difficult moments of my life have resulted in growth. Struggle creates opportunity. So many amazing things came out of the rubble of destruction and setbacks. I learned to find purpose through the pain—opportunities from life's obstacles. Being able to flip a struggle to a blessing is where the richness of life lies.

I started getting up at 5:00 a.m. to have my alone space to read and frame my day. I started getting more done every day than ever before. I used the early morning hours to work on writing—specifically this book. What used to seem like a productive day was now my morning. I became motivated and driven—everything was "all systems go."

I also wanted to push myself physically, so I entered a Spartan Race and trained like a savage every Sunday. I proudly worked up to doing thirty pull-ups and a hundred push-ups straight with no break—while slowly improving my less-than-impressive running pace.

Spartan Races are intense. The race I run is 10 kilometers up hills; through mud; navigating multiple monkey bars; carrying buckets, sandbags, and atlas stones; army crawls; in all, twenty-five obstacles. If you don't complete an obstacle, it's thirty burpees. I usually end up doing at least ninety burpees. It's a measure of character that tests your mental and physical strength and ability to push forward no matter how uncomfortable you feel. I was a bit intimidated by the race and the possibility of doing hundreds of burpees if I didn't complete the obstacles, but I did it. If you want a true test of your inner grit, sign up for one. I dismissed these races as gimmicky till I did it. I assure you, they are not in any way cheesy; these races are life-changing.

Negative people were out. Nights getting shit-faced for no reason were out. I couldn't waste any time just hanging out. Growing and building were too important to me. More albums to make, the circle would grow, the house would improve, and every day would build on the last. That's it.

I had my dad come over to assess the water damage. After he hobbled down the basement studio stairs—about to have a knee and ankle replaced—he told me, "Ben, if you have to build the studio back, then you should make it better." I get chills writing that. This comment was our life. The fire took our house, but we built another. The earthquake took our home, so we found a better one and fixed it. My Malibu didn't run, so I got a new motor and returned it to life. My house was broken when we bought it, and we fixed it up. Once again, we were taking the bad, flipping it, and improving it.

With the help of Dante—a lifelong family friend who feels more like an uncle or brother—we started ripping out the old and making more space for the new. For a moment, it was a return to the tribe of the motorcycle days. Dante was raised in the shop. He worked there since he was barely a teenager. He still held fond memories of growing up in the motorcycle culture. I loved hearing the stories about those days. It helped me understand what would have been if all hadn't been lost. A life that I never got to experience.

Dante, my dad, and I were making it happen. Not since I was five years old, at the motorcycle shop, had we spent so much time together. We were working to restore my space. The music studio is sacred to me like the garage is to them. They were helping me get my "shop" back—allowing me to return to my place of creation.

My dad was in immense pain and could barely walk, but we were doing what we had done for so long. I flashed on the tree fort—my first personal space. We were turning tragedy into gold, handling it ourselves, and creating a sanctuary where I could get lost in the music. We created the studio I had always dreamed of. Not elaborate and fancy, but private, concrete-walled and undisturbed by the outside world. A space where I made every song from then on, where I wrote this book, and where my grandfather's chair now sits.

As we rebuilt our home, I read and grew in various ways. I continued training for a Spartan Race once a week with my friend TK, a retired pro basketball player and coach, and his brother, an accomplished athlete. These sessions were vital to growth. To have a group that trained to the limits—once a week—was excellent for my body, mind, and soul. Also, they were like me—positive-minded—and liked to read inspirational books. There were not a lot of complainers in my developing friendship circle. The "poor me" attitude had no place at the table.

As my self-esteem continued to rise, my moves became more courageous. I took self-initiative in music and started contacting artists I liked—asking if they wanted to collaborate. Craigy-T of T.O.K. was happy to voice on my tune "Close 2 the Peace." I was so proud that a song I had self-produced was good enough for someone of Craigy-T's caliber to want to sing on. This positive feedback boosted my momentum to keep climbing.

To be clear, I was not smiling and smelling roses all day. My life was very chaotic during this time. I was on school drop-off and pick-up duty, selling houses, getting groceries, cooking, making music, and being a general contractor for our home remodel. Further, our dog, Luna, had a significant health issue and was slowly dying. She had a rare, incurable fungus that was gradually eating away her spine. I was very overworked and facing health issues. Anxiety was just under the surface, and heart palpitations and back aches were prevalent. Now, I had my positive anchors to keep me strong. My wins of the day were enough to give me the strength to persevere.

I finished painting our kitchen and my music studio late in the night—the remodel was done. I lay down, exhausted from working savagely on the finishing touches. I felt a little off. The next day, I started feeling worse. Mentally, everything felt off, too. I kept Gianna home because I couldn't even deal with driving her the two miles to school. This was Gianna's last school day before COVID-19 shut everything down for many months. Turns out I had COVID. The following weeks were brutal. My lungs were wrecked, and I felt horrible. I suffered from nausea, was out of breath, tired, and was just off. Everything in real estate became suspended. I couldn't even go collect my lockboxes on the listings. There were no showings and no income to bring in. Life stopped.

I needed to set up everything at home. The completion of the home remodel was perfectly timed for being in quarantine. I bought a pull-up bar online on the first day, figuring that if the isolation was longer than a few days, I needed to be able to keep up my fitness. Also, I went to my parents' house in the mountains and collected the weights I needed to maintain my fitness. These were the same weights we collected after the fire in my childhood. The same weights I lifted to get strong in my teen years. They even showed their rusted past again, as the paint had faded.

These weights came out of my great-uncle George's gym in downtown San Jose in the 1950s and then were at our house in the Santa Cruz Mountains until the fire in 1985. They sat rusty for a few years until I was thirteen and started lifting seriously. I sandblasted them and painted them black, which is their current look. The set has 50 lbs. standard plates, not 45 lbs.—for all my lifters. This is a rare thing I haven't seen many other places, due to the deliberate defiance of the metric system.

Since life was on pause, I could focus on what mattered—family, mental health, fitness, and music. I was able to give music a dedication I had never experienced before. All day could be given to creation. I didn't have to wear multiple hats, at least not professionally. I could focus on music like it was my full-time job. I could live in the creative space like I had always wanted to since my days at sound engineering school. I could spin the chaos of the lockdown into a time of creative focus—one that I always dreamed of. It was yet another example of purpose through the obstacles of life.

With this extra time, I could connect with musicians more. Specifically, my friend Dino and I started working on some music remotely. We would connect daily and discuss various ways to improve the songs I was working on. We started with a song I eventually titled "Soul." The daily song collaborations were essential to help get through COVID. These moments of focusing on the extreme details in a song helped me hear new layers in music. With Dino's help, the reverb volume came down. I mixed a drier vocal than I typically had been comfortable with. Dino pushed the next level of my authentic voice, which was much needed and appreciated.

During quarantine, our dog Luna got closer to death by the day, and nights were filled with terrifying yelps of pain if she moved even the smallest amount—abruptly waking us in the middle of the night. It was strange not to hear them any longer after she passed. Every day, I contemplated when that final moment would come. The doctors had said almost a year before that putting her down would be understandable. I wasn't hearing that. I wanted to give her every moment I could. I followed my instincts. I wanted to wait till I was confident it was time. She needed to experience all she could in her small amount of time on this planet.

I remember years earlier, I had a cat that had mouth cancer. I took him to the vet when his mouth developed into a big open wound, dripping blood everywhere. He started purring as we waited outside the clinic as I held him. He was happy and seemed not currently in pain. A few minutes later, the doctor recommended putting him down. I agreed and held him as he took his last breath. When it was over, as I drove away, the situation didn't sit well with me. I knew he had more life that he could have lived. Maybe only a few days or a week, but I feel everyone deserves to live as long as possible. I took this hard and carried the lesson of making sure I was confident it was time from that moment on.

With my previous experience with animals, I was comforted knowing we, as a family, could be with Luna during her dying days. She was getting worse, though, and there was a moment when I took her on her final walk around the neighborhood that I just knew she couldn't do it again. She still looked up at me, happy but in pain at the same time. I cried as we walked down the neighborhood trail for the last time, knowing that it would be the last time she could leave the property. She hadn't passed, but this was a significant moment in her decline. She was reduced to walking around our home and backyard.

The last moments in life are incredibly impactful. The final goodbye, the last kiss, graduation day, and the last game playing a sport you love—they all have an inevitable reality about human existence. The last moments remind us of life's impermanence, whether with a pet or a family member or friend—that final interaction sticks. The same applies to leaving jobs or moving out of a familiar house. I try to take a little extra reflection. I take it farther—when I stay in a hotel, I take a picture of the room as I'm leaving—a quick remembrance of the time and routine I lived by while living within those walls. I don't tend to ever look at these pictures, but they help me feel that moment of conclusion and that I take a little bit of the experience with me—a mental snapshot of times gone by.

The reminders of life's impermanence are sometimes very remarkable. Kendo was accepted into UC Berkeley with a major in astrophysics, and from that moment forward, the conclusion of his childhood was imminent. I was somewhat naïve about the monumental change that would occur in my life, but at the time, I was focused on the pride I felt in his accomplishment. On a paternal level, I couldn't help but find strength in the value I had given him to nurture his progress in life.

As August 2020 came around, I watched my son pack his things for college. He sighed in the middle of his room as his possessions were packed in his car. This was it. He stood next to his bed, and I took a picture, documenting the final time my son would be standing in his room—it became known as the office or guest room from then on.

While standing there, he held a whale-stuffed animal called Shuka, which we had gotten for him at Six Flags Discovery Kingdom when he was five. He loved it and slept with it every night at our house. Finally, Kendo said, "I don't care about anything else, Dad. Just leave Shuka in here." And with that, he put Shuka down on his desk, and we said our goodbyes. We stood outside as he got in his car and left as a resident of our home for the last time. We all watched him drive away until the taillights were out of sight.

As I walked back inside, eighteen years of raising Kendo raced through my mind. Eighteen years of long drives, great conversations, lifting weights, playing one-on-one basketball, and intense NBA 2K games had concluded. He was off to college. Things would now be different. I was extremely happy for him, but simultaneously, there was an instant void. Up to that point, he was with me my whole adult life. I knew it was time when he walked around the house just before he left. He was a man, and you could see in his demeanor that he needed freedom—independence was calling. But still, that change is a tough one to handle.

I gained a new appreciation for the time spent in Gianna's youth. I can picture the day Gianna leaves home, and Angela and I are a couple living alone. A middle-aged couple watching those taillights once again fade in the distance as life changes instantly.

I wanted to give Gianna all I could so she would be ready to enter the world fearlessly—with a tool kit for life. Also, I was beginning to see a distinct artistic talent blossom in her. She gravitated toward art in everything she did. In a striking moment, I realized she had an exceptional talent for singing after asking her to sing an "ah" sound in falsetto for a song I was working on with Dino. Her voice was distinct, authentic, and beautiful. I felt an obligation to help her with artistic progression. It seemed she had the perfect combination of nature and nurture when it came to singing.

We always sang in the car, like my mom and me when I was young, and she had an incredible ability to pitch unique harmony and flow patterns. I assume you think this is a dad talking, but trust me, I'm wearing my music producer hat when I say this—she has had the "it" factor from her earliest days. I think the seeds of our talents reveal themselves in our earliest days. So, with a broad brush, our interests and skills start emerging around five years old. The caveat to this statement is we must be exposed to things that interest us—exposure, talent, hard work, and desire—the combination that plants the seeds of success.

The seed of business ownership was always in my blood, so when I went for a morning walk and Pops called and said he wanted to leave our current brokerage and start our own, I was more than ready to begin the next chapter. I told him, "Okay. But if we do this, we must do it right—pro level." I feared being that low-grade brokerage with a lousy logo that looked like they sold birdhouses. I was excited about the idea of our own thing, but I was also happy with our current brokerage, Sereno Group. I liked Sereno, and one of the founders, Chris, was always striving for greatness and brought out the best in people. He was also the office manager who interviewed me when I joined Coldwell Banker so many years ago. However, I knew it was time to move on. My father and I had independent ambitions and a fast-ticking timeline.

Independent entrepreneurship—those words alone spark excitement in me. My father was now seventy, and it was time. I didn't want to feel regret for not doing what we had always talked about. Soon, this possibility would no longer exist, so we needed to act. It was time to be courageous and take control of our real estate business.

Finding Purpose Through Pain

Don't wait for perfect conditions. That's how dreams die in the waiting room—stuck in the "once this happens" mindset. Create through the chaos. Progress is available daily, not just when life is easy or you have endless amounts of free time. The timing will never be right—create regardless of how you feel or what you have going on.

I recorded "Rolling Stone" in a dining room full of boxes, appliances, and dust while my family was going on with their lives around me. It didn't matter. I was reclaiming my voice. I was done waiting. Don't wait. Engage in your progress immediately.

Reinvention is a part of the process, and there is beauty in forming the new chapter. You will need to reinvent yourself often and begin new chapters in your journey. As time goes by, setbacks and difficult transitions are signals to transform and rise again with new aspects of you. My studio rebuild was a symbolic moment that mirrored my past with fires and earthquakes. We took the setback, dealt with the chaos, and made it better than before. This mentality is in my blood. The old is ruined—build it back better. With your hands, if you need to. Just get it done.

Strength comes from having anchors in your life. When the storms of life hit, you will endure. Reading, fitness, music, family are not hobbies—they are lifelines to stay grounded. Double down on your anchors when things get rough. I started getting up at 5:00 a.m. to read and write when the studio was not available. That one shift changed everything. Now I read over seventy-five books every year.

Time with loved ones is fleeting; embrace that time we have with an understanding that it is all impermanent. There will be a last conversation. The relationships you have will change over time. Parents age and children become adults—relationships are not static. They evolve and change constantly, although sometimes slowly enough not to notice. When you look back, what brings peace is knowing you gave your loved ones your time and let them know how much they mattered to you.

No one is coming to hand you a better chapter in life. You write it through your actions and decisions. You rebuild it when it's broken.

CHAPTER 21

WAY TO BE

Am I destined for—greatness, or will I just fall short? Fakeness, or will I keep it real? Broken, or will I just heal? Am I destined for greatness?

"*Way to Be*"

On January 12, 2021, I started the day in my garage doing cardio. Luna was lying by me as I finished up on the elliptical machine. Then I left for Hayward. I had a home inspection for one of my listings when Angela called me and said Luna was falling over—she couldn't walk, and her eyes had rolled back in her head. While the home inspector climbed onto the roof to take a look, I checked the backyard camera I had set up at home to see the traumatic event unfold. It was chilling. She took her last steps, and her back gave out. I told the inspector I needed to go immediately and called Kendo, and he met me at the house so we could all be there with Luna.

When I got home, Luna was in bad shape. She couldn't walk or stand and was in unbearable pain. We sat on a blanket with her in the backyard, looking at the sky for about an hour. These were the last hours of Luna's life, and I wanted to show her as much love as possible. Once it felt right, Kendo and I carried her in the blanket to the car. Kendo and Gianna said their final goodbye with tear-filled eyes, and then Angela and I started Luna's final drive while the kids stayed home. Angela and I drove silently to the hospital to perform the inevitable fate we had known was coming for a year. After Luna got wheeled into the pet hospital on a gurney, the doctor started prepping for the end. I put my head down against hers as the doctor injected the medicine. As I petted her, Angela repeatedly told Luna we loved her. Luna licked my face as she took her last breaths. It was not a happy lick. It was her way of saying, "I love you, Ben. Thank you for loving me back."

We entered the hospital, the three of us. We left just two. I looked at the fur Luna had left on the carpeted wall of my car's backseat. Just a few moments before she was alive. I kept her fur there for over a year. I wasn't ready to let it go.

Some things never leave us. Our connections with animals remain strong even decades after they have passed. I take comfort in knowing we did everything possible for Luna. Luna, we will always love you, and you will never be forgotten. I appreciate every minute we got to spend together.

The next day, my dad called and said my great-uncle Jim was very sick and suggested I contact him. Uncle Jim lived life to the fullest—I looked up to him. He was an accountant, played some pro baseball for the San Francisco Seals, started companies with Willie Mays, and even helped organize boxing events with Muhammad Ali. He also had an eclectic group of friends and clients—including Carol Doda, one of the first and most voluptuous topless dancers in San Francisco.

Jim helped my dad at the beginning of the motorcycle business days, and he loved to support those who went after what they wanted in life. I looked up to Jim like a grandfather and mentor since I didn't have many memories of my dad's dad. Also, whenever Jim came around to family functions, we played catch, and he would sit and talk with me and ask me how things were going. He also played accordion and was sharp as a tack into his nineties. I asked Jim once what he attributed to being so active late in life. He said, "I'm always curious and always learning." Curiosity seemed to do the trick—that and eating dandelion leaves—the combination was quite successful.

Jim died two days after Luna. He was the last connection to the generation before my parents, and now that had reached its conclusion. That whole generation, in my life at least, was gone. They lived on in their accomplishments and stories passed down to future generations.

I felt like a baton had been passed—it was my time to carry on and push forward toward greatness. The handoff from one generation to another was occurring. I was now forty and becoming the paternal guide. I was now a man who was a third-generation descendant of my grandfather, George (Juro) Barbic, who immigrated from the island of Lastovo (Lagosta) in Croatia in the early 1900s. I had met my great-grandfather when I was very young. Hopefully, I can live long enough to become a great-grandfather. Also, I dream of returning to the land that started it all —a family trip to Lastovo to see where one courageous decision set in motion generations of progress. I want to picture where my grandfather stood when he decided to leave his island for a place with more opportunities.

I often think of the immigrant journey in my family, or any family—that moment they said goodbye to family and friends for the last time. I think of the moment they set off to explore the unknown. Immigrants are the ultimate travelers down the unknown road in life. I take inspiration from my grandparents on both sides of my family, who left all they had ever known and never looked back. In those days, it was a long journey by boat, and communication was only by mail. Compared to what I have experienced, they were the true heroes. Those who came before us faced hardships of a much more significant nature. Our comfort can be a blessing and a curse. Having an appreciation for what we have is vital to understanding how much we are capable of—all that past generations endured so we can be in this world now.

I started writing my story alone in an airport two hours before my flight to a show I was to perform. I began writing on my phone, then my laptop, casually starting from the beginning of my life. I wanted to document my memories and keep a journal. I aimed to write down my life and eventually share it with my kids, hoping they could draw inspiration from it. I did not intend to publish a book, but something noteworthy emerged on the pages. I recognized common threads and experiences that helped me endure and continue to climb in life. I noticed patterns and skills that I had picked up. I discovered my ability to turn pain into purpose and always push forward. As I continued documenting my life, I became more of a writer and a reader, which stemmed from a very organic place. I never really decided to be a writer—it just happened organically.

This book was initially about my journey in music, but it became so much more. It became my past, present, and future. It became my "how-to" book for living a meaningful life. It became my therapy when I needed to get something out. Finally, it became the portal to a new endeavor I was determined to finish. My story was about the journey, how I got here, and where I was going next.

As I wrote the book, I gained a deeper understanding of myself, my music, and what inspires me lyrically. I had my musical catalog fresh in my mind, having written the book and incorporated the songs, so I created a demo reel showcasing many of my best musical moments. Within a few days of sending it to various producers, I got a text from Adonis.

Adonis Shropshire has production credits at the highest level, working with artists like Mariah Carey, Usher, and Chris Brown, and has been nominated for a remarkable seventeen Grammys. It tripped me out to be talking to someone with a resume like his; it was a level-up moment. He saw the potential and wanted to work with me, so we got to work after a quick negotiation. I sent him "Close 2 Peace" as a reference, and he dug right into making the riddim.

While I was driving in the car with Kendo, Adonis sent me the draft of what became "Last Call." Kendo and I listened to it and understood this was real—I was working with Adonis. It wasn't "maybe" or "someday" we would do a project—I had the song in my inbox. I worked on the vocals for this song for about a week, sent it to Adonis, and he agreed: it was ready to be mixed. After officially adding him to my biography as a producer I'd worked with,

I could pivot once again, pushing forward my progress in music with ever-increasing confidence.

I had a challenging two weeks, where I took a rusty screwdriver through the hand while trying to pry open Gianna's jewelry box. Unfortunately, it got infected from the rust, swelling up quite large and requiring antibiotics. Then, three days later on my bike, I collided head-on with another biker in my lane on a downhill blind turn. I drove my bike home with immense pain from the handlebars going into my stomach—eventually giving me a permanent scar. I was on antibiotics and in considerable pain over the coming days, but I channeled my discomfort into the writing. The recording helped me with the pain. I learned to use discomfort to my advantage. It was empowering to know I could overcome this. I didn't let setbacks take me off of my path.

"Way to Be" again flowed out honestly and effortlessly. I worked on the mix for two consecutive days, making incremental changes and tweaks. I was evolving closer to my genuine truth as an artist. The book—and life—was inching me closer to the truth that was inside. The hopelessness of panic and disasters was no longer present. I had experienced feeling good and refused to return to the darkness of my past. I wanted to distance myself further from the pain and chaos I once felt. I believe this is part of my inner drive—to never return to the darkness. To never feel the weight of the evil, universal energy creeping on me, lurking to take me out spontaneously. I had armor—confidence and courage. I was almost ready to stand tall and embrace my wounds of the past.

Finding Purpose Through Pain

Love is proven in the final moments. Being present for a loved one, whether it's a pet, family member, or friend, is the most sacred responsibility you can hold. When you are able to be with someone through the final moments, you can honor who they are and what they gave you.

It is not easy, but I held Luna during her final breaths and told Jim what an inspiration he was to me a day before he passed. I printed his response email and it hangs on the wall of the staircase to my studio, a reminder of the generational handoff and the respect I pay to my ancestors as I progress forward.

Loss and pain can be the turning points if you meet them with courage and understanding. They contain the insight for growth, clarity, and a more authentic version of yourself. The most powerful personal transformation can come when everything seems to be falling apart. Create through the chaos, self-reflect, and trust that the pain can be shaped into purpose.

Eventually, the baton will get passed to you—will you be ready? The generation before you will fade, and it becomes your turn. It is what you build, how you build it, how you love, and the courage you show in difficult times that others will see and potentially follow. Live with clarity, create with honesty, and hold your values high, and you can be steady when the world shakes.

CHAPTER 22

MOMENT 2 MOMENT

FRANKIE NOW HAD A podcast, *Moment 2 Moment*, and I was one of the first guests. The day I was to go on, I was intimidated—I had no idea what to expect. It was a long-format interview, meaning it wasn't a five-minute conversation but was to run over forty-five minutes. It felt surreal that one of my oldest and best friends was interviewing me. As Frankie began, he brought up my past—the highs and lows. He brought up catching cases (arrests). I had never publicly talked about this stuff because I was always ashamed. It was this weight I had on my shoulders. As I was talking, I was concerned about what people were going to think. I carried this worry for a few weeks after the interview concluded, fearful of being judged.

I remember sitting at my kitchen table thinking, *What would our friends who are cops think?* That thought stirred something deep inside. Shame tried to creep in, the same shame I'd carried for years, but this time, something shifted. I didn't shrink. I sat with the weight of my past, and instead of running from it, I stood in it. I honored this part of my story for the first time. I realized that if someone could only be my friend while I hid my truth, then that was never friendship to begin with. That thought flipped something in me.

I told myself, *I'm proud of who I am. I embrace every step that brought me here. I'm ready for what's next—unapologetically.* For the first time in my life, I felt free—free of shame, free of hiding. My story wasn't something to conceal; it was something to carry with pride. From that point forward, I knew I had to share it—through conversations, podcasts, or this book—openly, completely, and without apology. Because the truth became a new narrative, I'm not afraid of where I've been. And I'm not hiding from any of it anymore.

Frankie's podcast was groundbreaking in my personal development. I later found out my interview was one of the most listened to of all his podcasts. The validation helped me feel that I had something worthwhile to say. It was time to let the world know me—and finish my book. I had started this book long before the podcast, but after I did the interview, I was okay with telling my whole story.

Without this moment, you probably would never have read my book. I probably wouldn't have ever had the courage to tell my whole story, to get a literary agent, and to publish my book with one of the most influential and far-reaching publishers around.

This interview was a turning point in my life, not because something massive changed outside me, but because I finally let the inside of me be seen without filters. I stopped hiding from who I was. It was after this interview that I reedited the book countless times, giving more of myself in the process.

When I sat down with one of my oldest friends on the *Moment 2 Moment* podcast, I didn't know I was walking into a moment of liberation. I had never publicly spoken about my arrests or the darker chapters of my life. I'd carried shame, quietly afraid it might taint the way people saw me. But as the conversation unfolded, I realized hiding was a prison, and truth was the key.

The fear didn't vanish overnight. I questioned everything afterward. But one thought shifted everything: *If someone only respects me when I hide who I am, they don't really respect me at all.* It's all based on a front, a misguided, fraudulent presentation of who I am. That's when I decided to stop editing my life for others. I began to see my past not as baggage, but as ballast—something that kept me steady, grounded, and real. Something that I could use to connect me to others going through a similar experience. I could help others climb by showing how I did it.

And the response? People didn't reject me. They connected. That validation didn't stroke my ego—it strengthened my voice. It gave me permission to improve and finish my book, to speak more boldly, to live out loud. I was free of the self-induced shame of the past.

Finding Purpose Through Pain

The moment you stop hiding is the moment your real life begins. When you stop asking for approval and start telling the truth, people don't run—they lean in. It takes a whole lot of courage to lead with your truth. It's vulnerable, and the potential for attack rises. What I found is that when you stop pretending or hiding from who you truly are, you can finally attract what you desire most. Musically, professionally, and romantically, leading with the truth makes people connect.

People can feel it when you "put on" and create a false narrative. When you are genuine, all of life becomes more enjoyable. You tell people, "I am comfortable with who I am." It is through countless hours of inner work and moments of vulnerability that your true self can emerge—you can shine bright. To stand tall and be okay standing out in your truth.

Shame thrives in silence. It can dull your inner flame and prevent the life you deserve. When you can tell the truth out loud, that is when the weight you have carried—arrests, shame, fear of judgment—can be released. Decide not to run from it anymore. Find strength in who you are, not the mistakes you have made.

What I learned that day on the *Moment 2 Moment* podcast is something I hope you can take with you. Hiding from your past doesn't protect you—it imprisons you. If someone only respects a filtered, inauthentic version of you, then they never respected you in the first place—it was all an illusion.

The moment that you stop hiding is the moment your real life begins. People won't always reject you; they will see themselves in you. That is the purpose of this book and my personal evolution to get to the point of putting my life story out to the world. Share with others. Have the conversations on a deeper level. There is so much we have in common that without real conversation, we will never know. You are not alone, so be a voice that helps champion in connection in a time that needs it so desperately.

CHAPTER 23

LAST CALL

Do you feel life giving you all you wanted and then some? No time, and we flying to thrive though. Where you from don't mean where you are now. You a star, and you rise when you fall down. Growth feeling, more meaning and soul, and then. Oh seed that I sow, take hold, no pretend.

"Endless Summer"

KENDO WAS NOW A young man on his path, and my guidance would be less prominent, with more telephone calls than in-person time. I felt happiness and sadness that our relationship was in the next phase. The reality was that I was now a father of a grown-up son. That's a trip for a forty-year-old man. I began thinking of the next phase in life—the time after the kids leave the house. Parenting was a big part of my life for so long. I gained a lot on this journey to share. Soon, it would be my time to start wearing a new hat, with a chance to share and help others beyond the family unit. I wanted to show others what I had gained about shining brightly through the darkest moments, about rising tall and proud. I always circle back to being happy in the darkest of times—feelings like a summer afternoon when it's storming, dark, and cold. I wrote "Endless Summer" with that exact concept in mind. I was pushing through the dark times and making purpose out of pain.

What would your ideal day look like? How far are you from experiencing it? What steps could be taken to achieve your goal? Does your voice inside echo the dream-killing advice of friends and family? Do you think you are worth it? Do you deserve to live your ideal day, your ideal life?

I have become passionate about instilling the ideal self or the perfect day concept in others, especially my kids, friends, and family. Optimized versions of ourselves are a fascinating concept to me. How close can we get to our ideal selves at any period of our lives? Constantly searching for what we are capable of in all categories.

In 2008, while holding my teddy bear made by Angela and Kendo, I decided I would take control and keep pushing. I decided to be the man they thought I was. Every day, I keep going. I continually strive for goals in all that I do, always pushing myself to climb higher. I stumble all the time. I lose track, lose focus, and feel the time is slipping away, but I always bounce back. Those moments of emptiness and unfulfillment don't last. The rejections and setbacks don't last either. The things that didn't pan out were vital for my progress. My early trauma was critical to my progress.

Here is what I have come to realize. All the best in me (or us as humans) comes from these moments. When you're told "No!" you can say "Fuck that shit!" and make it great. Prove them wrong. These painful and emotional knocks fuel and propel us forward. These knockdown moments will be part of what makes life better and stronger—if you take control.

When I finally got the mix back for "Last Call," I realized I hadn't been authentic with Adonis. I was intimidated by his status in the music industry and hadn't revealed my true self. I was reserved, and I didn't create from the heart. I sought guidance from him instead of using my years in music to maximize the art. I gave up control to him, and he didn't want it. The song did okay, even charting in a few countries, but I look back on what it could have been—what I could have done to take fuller advantage of the opportunity.

I rushed the tune because I was so excited to work with Adonis. I didn't listen to my instincts, flustered by the thoughts of grandeur due to his resume. The best way to summarize the experience is a project without a leader. The expectation of the collaboration was far grander than the reality of "Last Call." I didn't shine bright. I was comfortable standing in the shadows. I didn't follow the state of mind that has always pushed me forward, but I learned a lesson. Be me. Shine bright. Be okay standing tall and being seen.

Accepting reality is sometimes difficult to handle. Think about what it felt like when you didn't make the sports team, didn't get the promotion you wanted or the part in the musical you sought. Whether loss or setback, try not to fear rejection, no matter how difficult. Embrace it. Thank the critic in your life for helping to open your eyes and become a better version of yourself.

Level up. Hitting new milestones brings so much satisfaction to the self. Watch as you connect with people from the past—something feels different. Those who used to seem strong are now weaker. Those who seemed happy in the past now don't seem that content. Those who seemed successful in the past might not have continued their path. I say this cautiously, though. I am not trying to put a "better than thou" message out there. It's just that we can see progress as we grow. As my skill developed, I became sensitive to the nuances in music—I could hear the flaws.

Subtle improvements are a fun part of growth. As you grow, you resonate with different people. Love the journey. Love the process and goals you set. Now, everywhere I go, it's different. I'm not that asshole who is always smiling and whistling. But I am that guy on a mission. I know how I want to fill my day, and I live every day excited about the next. And I'm happy that's the life I carved out for myself.

As the quarantine from 2020 lessened, I sat in my first open house in almost two years. It was a refreshing moment. I realized all the personal development I had achieved from these open houses. After nearly eighteen years in real estate, I realized how much personal growth I had gained by dealing with people. I met different people and saw their personality differences. I never treated people as customers but as guests—welcoming them into my home. They relaxed when I showed them the house rather than feeling pressured that I was trying to sell it to them. I knew they might want me to represent them if they liked me. If it is mutual, then we have a match. Above all others, this activity brought me out of my cocoon.

When I was twenty-three years old, sitting in these open houses, it was evident that I was intimidated by the experience. I was a wounded young man. The buyers and sellers were older and more successful than I was. But gradually, as I worked relentlessly on personal growth, I started enjoying meeting new people. Instead of the jarring, flustered feeling of the door opening in my early twenties, I was now excited to meet people and talk with them. I was able to be genuine—not a plastic salesman. Real estate prepared me for all the other activities in music and life ahead. I dealt with people's life savings and took that responsibility very seriously. I'm not money-driven at all. I value quality experiences.

Also, I saw how some realtors barely held on to their clients. It validated my philosophy and approach. Some real estate agents are intimidated by the confident, grounded sort. It's funny to watch them try to maintain the inauthentic shtick when you try to be yourself with no hidden agenda. But just like high-level musicians, good agents see eye to eye.

I would try frantically to stay afloat if I were just in music. In some ways, that would be good, but more than likely, it would require some compromises. This way, through real estate, I never have to throw in the towel on my music career. I can focus on the art and the craft and never need to say, "Time to get a day job." My lifestyle is sustainable, and I love every day that I have. I never had to give up on the thing I loved. I could always get better at it. Some music full-timers don't have a "career" to fall back on and don't have the flexibility I have. I carved out the perfect situation. I got into real estate nineteen years prior because I had a son to raise. The real estate industry helped keep my musical dreams alive. These two worlds fit perfectly for who I am and the skills I've developed.

We set aside our passions when faced with that "grow-up" moment. When we do that, we die a little inside—and death becomes a slow decline. Various aspects of our lives slowly deteriorate. If we don't make a solid commitment to growing every day, we can only do the opposite of that. I've seen too many people I used to hang with slowly dying inside. Joy becomes lost. Passion dies, and a love of life also goes.

Remember this: Our children get more from our actions than from anything else. They take note of our mental state. They notice if their parents are happy, sad, depressed, driven, resentful, or hateful. If we don't remain true to our actual selves, we experience an internal conflict—and our children can sense that struggle. When you meet a person in alignment, there is a different energy. You can feel it. Life might hit them hard, but they don't give excuses. They climb out of the dirt and keep going.

Love passion. Love spontaneity. Love doing the things that intimidate or scare you. How many decisions and moves are you not making out of fear? I want to squeeze every ounce out of life before I die. Then, on that final day, I want to grin with accomplishment. I want to feel I gave everything I could to my wife, kids, and parents. I want to feel like I sang every song I had in me. I want to have written every word I could before my brain loses its cognitive ability. I want to run every race and lift every heavy weight I can. I will maximize everything I can. I refuse to live any other way and will ensure I do this for the rest of my days.

Finding Purpose Through Pain

Life constantly evolves, and your roles do as well. Each new phase offers a doorway for either growth or withering. Nothing remains in one position. Things are either growing or deteriorating at all times. Keep growing toward the most fulfilled and valuable version of yourself.

Your most painful moments can become the source of your greatest strength. When pain is almost unbearable, the fuel within it can burn the most intensely. Use the uncomfortable, difficult times to push forward with the help of the pain it contains.

The youth of the world learn from who you are, not what you say. It might be cliché to say that, but what is not cliché is this: It goes way beyond what you do or say. If you abandon your own dreams, the youth will inherit the disconnection you contain toward that which you love. If you pursue purpose with fire and focus, then without saying anything, you will be giving them the permission to do the same. This can be applied to your own children or any youth who are in your life or watching your actions.

Having multiple passions or income streams isn't weak. You might have to have a day job and sacrifice to survive and provide. Regardless, build a life that protects and holds your purpose sacred. Don't let the inner momentum lose fuel and die out due to responsibilities. Become more focused and hold the time spent pursuing what you love in the highest regard.

CHAPTER 24

COURAGE & BRAVERY

Working so hard, and now the dead weight gone so. Don't sit still, go the unknown road. Foundation built strong indeed. Courage and bravery inside me.

"Courage & Bravery"

When I began writing, I wanted to document my life. I tried to get everything down to record my life's adventures, index my timeline, and show what a ride I've been on. As I finished writing the original draft, I asked a few people in my inner circle to read my manuscript and enjoyed their emotional connection to my story. I was so new to writing that finishing a first draft was quite an accomplishment. I found it amazing that people who were part of my initial musical journey over twenty years prior could now be the first readers in my next chapter in life. Finally, I thought I was ready to share with those close to me and even people I didn't know.

I wasn't prepared for criticism when the subject was my life. I sent the manuscript for book analysis, and after getting it back, I was filled with anger at the response. But really, that anger was just masking the vulnerability underneath. They said it was good but needed a lot of work—too much name-dropping and stories of no importance. I felt like I had been attacked, not just in the layout and narrative of my book, but in the very core of who I was.

I had given my life as an open book and was naïve to the fact that I had just started writing—this was my first song again. When I sent the manuscript to the initial review team, I instinctively knew what I wanted. I was asking for permission to keep the weak lines. I sought permission to keep it sloppy and not put in the extra time. I tried to ignore the fact that my writing had just begun. I wanted someone to tell me "Good job," but it wasn't warranted.

The fact was, I was still sensitive to sharing my life story. The wounds were still fresher than I realized. The details now present were not in the original draft—I wasn't ready to dive deep into the emotional side of my life. I needed to slowly accept that if I was writing a book about my life, I couldn't cheat the reader or myself. After a few weeks, I realized what needed to be done. I accepted how far my writing needed to go.

I edited the manuscript daily, peeling back the layers to uncover the underlying truth in my life, reading every morning about the writing process, and discovering the common thread that runs through my life. I found that lessons and struggles repeatedly appear in my life. I saw the importance of courage and bravery in moving forward with my life story.

Writing and completing a book takes courage—the courage needed to stick with your goals. It takes bravery to combat any ridicule or criticisms while exposing all your life's darkest and brightest moments. It takes follow-through to keep going and stop at nothing until completion. Additionally, it requires reviewing your life and identifying the thread of consistency you encountered and faced at every step of your journey.

The final song released while writing this book was "Courage & Bravery."

For me, the theme repeated consistently throughout my life is taking control. We can't always control what happens to us, but we can control how we respond. We can take control of our path and not let distractions take us off course. Our houses can burn down, earthquakes can destroy our possessions, and homes can flood. It's on us to determine how we respond to those traumatic events. We can either take a "poor me" attitude or spin unfortunate events into lessons that strengthen us. I might have to drive over five hours on a Friday to be a part of my son's life, but I'm doing it. The result of this decision to choose personal responsibility goes beyond words. Things happen. Spin that shit into gold. Mistakes and failures happen. Learn and grow from them. Help others get through the same challenges.

Motivate, create, and live the life you want. If someone tells you you're too old, young, dumb, fat, lazy, etc., take control and create your reality. Use that doubt as fuel to push forward. I'm far from done. Every day is improving, and I refuse to have it any other way. Shit will happen. I know that. But I will squeeze every bit of life out of my journey—no regrets and plenty of mistakes.

As I drove my daughter on Highway 17 up the mountain to my childhood home, she started singing "On the Road Again" to herself. I asked her if an artist she liked sang the song. She said it was a Willie Nelson song. Instantly, I got chills. I had come full circle. We drove down the road to my parents' home, singing together—the same road I had taken countless times with my mom and dad in the old orange van. I passed all the redwood trees, still with the burnt bark from three decades prior, and explained to her that back when I was a small child, this whole forest had burned. I told her that redwood trees are resilient. "They can withstand a lot, like us." Finding purpose through pain and rising above the ashes.

CHAPTER 25

GRATEFUL

And I'm grateful, grateful, I'm grateful for the hard knock life . . .

"Grateful"

SINCE THE CLOSING PAGES of this story, I've entered a new season I call The Ascent. It's not just about climbing—it's about rising with clarity, mission, and meaning. I've been building something bigger than myself. My music continues to evolve, my real estate work supports my freedom, and my body stays strong through mountain trail runs and heavy lifting. But what's even more powerful is this: my voice, my message, and my truth are now fully aligned.

Now, I wake up each day building with even more enthusiasm and focus. Writing this book gave me the clarity to understand what was next. I'm writing new books. I'm mixing for global artists and performing with intention. I'm running trails, lifting with my son, dancing with my daughter, laughing with my wife, and pushing past any voice that says I'm too late or too much. As you know, I gave up on caring about that long ago.

So, as I speak to you, the reader, I want you to know I care. I want you to succeed. I want you to enjoy every moment of your time on this planet. I believe firmly in the pivot moment in life and that unending dedication to progress can help you overcome whatever life throws at you. I am beyond grateful that you read through my book. I am further excited to hear about your changes, what you are doing to push things forward and thrive.

This book is not a gimmick or a sermon. This is my life in its raw and true form. I commit to you that I will continue to give the same authentic life lessons and growth that I pick up along the way. As I'm sure you know by now, I don't stop. I have already written four hundred pages of my next book, and I'm just getting started.

This was just the first book, but not the last. I'll keep rising, keep building, and keep showing you what it means to live wide awake. I've found purpose through pain, and now I live by the code—rise and climb. I'm not here to fade out—I'm here to blaze through. The climb never ends—and neither do I.

I feel compelled to speak the truth and share one final point, not as a man who has finished climbing, but as someone who has learned that the climb never really ends.

When we chase greatness, it's easy to blur the line between dedication and destruction. What starts as a passion can, without warning, become a prison. I've seen it in my own life—how fitness, when pushed too far, can break the body. How clean eating, when driven by fear instead of strength, can erode joy. Striving for success, when rooted in comparison or insecurity, can silently drain the soul. We live in a culture that glorifies the grind. But I've learned that just because something is praised doesn't mean it's healthy. Just because it's admired doesn't mean it's sustainable.

We are allowed to rest. We are allowed to love ourselves at 70 percent capacity some days. We are allowed to seek help. We are allowed to let go of identities that no longer serve our spirit. Look around, yes—but don't look so long at others that you forget to see yourself. Comparison can be the thief of joy, but obsession is the thief of peace.

So if you've ever felt like you were losing yourself while trying to become more yourself, you're not alone. If you've ever pushed too hard, too fast, because the world made you feel like you were behind, so have I. If you've ever confused achievement with worth, I've done the same.

Let this be your reminder:

You are not behind. You are not broken. You are not late. You are not alone.

The journey is long. The climb is exciting. Rising with purpose is fulfilling. The spirit of a thriving life is sacred. And your worth is not tied to your wins. This book may be subtitled *Finding Purpose Through Pain*, but purpose doesn't mean perfection. It means truth. It means alignment. It means climbing—but climbing wisely. With compassion. With clarity. With care for the vessel carrying you.

And when you forget all that, as I often have, begin again. Acknowledge the moment and proceed.

That's the real rise. That's the climb that counts.

ACKNOWLEDGMENTS

THIS BOOK IS DEDICATED to the family that helped me on my journey. Without the love and support of the following people, I wouldn't be who or where I am.

Mom, you were my first supporter. You helped show me that the world is good and we can lead with love. You believed in me and showed me that I could achieve whatever I wanted. Dad, your ambition, intensity, and comfort with the uncomfortable helped me navigate the world. Your dedication to excellence framed the blueprint for my life.

Grandma and Grandpa Diehl, you were the love, stability, and support I desperately needed in childhood. Your smiles and enthusiasm made me appreciate what a loving family is. I feel your positive energy with me to this day.

Angela, you were there when I needed you, and you pushed me to be the man I am now. You believed in me. You have stood by me in my darkest days—and knew who I was. You showed me love and never tried to change me. I will always stand by you and am privileged to spend my life with you.

Kendo, you came into the world when I needed you the most. I could not ask for a better son, and watching you take flight in life is one of my greatest joys. I am very proud of the man you have become and the kindness and love in your heart.

Gianna, your passion and spirit brighten my day. Your creativity and courage inspire many, including me. You are wise beyond your years, and so much awaits your life journey.

Gianna and Kendo, in your darkest moments, remember your finest ones. I hope you can look back forty years from now and get a spark to push you through your day when reading this. Always have the courage to let the world know who you are—be you.

Additionally, I would like to thank my publisher at Skyhorse Publishing, Tony Lyons, who believed in my original manuscript and the truth it contained. Your trust helped bring this story into the world as it was meant to be told.

Thanks to my editor, Daniela Rapp, whose insight and skill guided the book's final transformation. Your encouragement to rewrite the "Purpose Through Pain" sections, along with your high-level feedback throughout, elevated the message and deepened its impact.

I'm grateful to my agent, Alan Morell at CMP, for believing in me as a first-time writer. Your steady counsel, belief, and representation paved the way to Skyhorse Publishing.

A special thanks to my dear friend and trusted guide, Frankie Ordoubadi, for helping me bring more of myself into these pages. Your honesty, energy, and words were crucial in helping me discover the most genuine version of this book.

Thanks also to Zack Reed at Rebel Sound Records for believing in this work from the very beginning—offering your time, edits, and support.

Gerri Knilans, thank you for your dedication during the early months of shaping the manuscript, teaching me copy editing, and helping me grow as a writer.

Finally, I would like to thank everyone who helped and encouraged me to write this book. The list is long, and I am always here for you, like you were for me.